MY FATHER'S GHOST IS SLEEPING ON THE STAIRS

Reflections of a Young Architect

MY FATHER'S GHOST IS SLEEPING ON THE STAIRS

Reflections of a Young Architect: A Memoir of a Life & a Time

BARDDRIEV PRESS

Copyright © Brad Drew 2019

All rights reserved

First Edition
Paperback

ISBN: 978-0-9944992-3-3

Apart from any fair dealing for the purposes of private study, research or review, as permitted under the Copyright Act, no part of this book may be reproduced by any process without permission. Copyright of all text and illustrations resides under the Copyright, Designs and Patents Act with Brad Drew.

Layout and Book Design: Brad Drew
Poetry, drawings and prints: Brad Drew
Photographs from the family archives of Brad Drew
Cover Art and Design: Brad Drew

MY FATHER'S GHOST IS SLEEPING ...

My Father's ghost is sleeping on the stairs;
The attic air is musty with his heat.
Heir to his chaptered blood,
I recognise the scent of reason's breath
And navigate the corridors that bleed
This sap of singularity – his heirs.

My Mother's brother's eyes gaze back from home,
To burn me through the confines of the glass.
With incandescent eye,
In mirrors and shop windows as I pass,
He mocks all futile efforts made to flee
The stamp of blood fixed firm within the stone.

My Mother keeps her silence to herself;
Just hums and smiles discretely from the hearth.
With patience and with love,
She stands aside, to murmur through the breath
Contained within the stone, the stair, the blood,
That all is as it should be – such is life.

Late afternoon's shafts filter through the slats;
Light up each mote of dust upon the sill:
Illumined shards long-gone,
Come present – gather likewise, for us all:
Reminders of the blood stored in the stone ...
My Father's ghost is stirring, as he sleeps upon the stairs.

Brad Drew © 27 July 2017

MY FATHER'S GHOST: A MEMOIR

IN THE BEGINNING
Was the word ... and as with most beginnings,
there has to come, at some point, an ending.

I set out, to make this beginning in the hope that my words
will make their journeys, across, up or down through the years and
eventually expend themselves
before there comes a time for my own ending ...
as come it must, to us all ... ...

There could, in these godlike times, eventually be exceptions to this.
???

I didn't amount to all that much, but
I did have some interesting moments getting there ...
And a parade of interesting, special people passed me by.

1

Beginnings

I SIT HERE AND REGARD my suddenly-parchmentlike skin and wonder how it has all managed to come down to this – my teeth, for a long time now, reduced to a certified minority group; my hair, intact but blindingly-snowlike and daily losing ground in the battle for substantiality; any muscle tone I possess, in spite of regular gym workouts, somehow displaying a flaccidity which I cannot remember as ever having been there earlier; my legs, which more and more remind me of Spike Milligan's own conversation with the 'Author' about his, in the opening to 'Puckoon' (a favourite gem for me, of long-ago youthful nostalgia); my own eyes, once brightly-blue, on every once an occasion, will stare back from the mirror as the rheumy grey eyes of a latter-day uncle of mine, now very much, long-dead. And finally, as I once again attempt to tune in my recently-acquired hearing aid, to such a level where myself and others sound almost something-approaching-normal (though by now, with the inevitable distortions ever-present in such devices, I feel I've forgotten what normal ever sounded like), I gain some small realisation as to why, in all the representations I've ever seen of him, Beethoven always manages to look so very, very angry ... (the miracle is that in spite of his deafness, he managed to continue to create such a glorious legacy using his mind's ear and the resonant vibrations of solid surfaces. Had someone presented him with an electronic hearing aid, he may in time have managed to appear even angrier).

    I sat quietly in the newly-fitted-out waiting-area of the larger of our local department stores today, waiting for my partner to return from the new change rooms with her probable purchase decided on. The entire shopping centre is currently in a total state of chaos, undergoing major extensions, including major refurbishments by most of the existing occupants. The store seemed in a state of limbo, with yawning gaps like lost teeth where endless stands of clothing used to be and a temporary air hanging confusingly over everything else. The upmarket, relocated change rooms were slick and moderne, with doors to booths held in gently curving lines, so as to recede from view in both directions like the interior of an alternate Tardis; all in a crisp styling of frosted glass set within black glossy metal frames, reminiscent of Japanese nouvelle. This waiting area formed a neat hub, with several comfortably-padded tub chairs and simple side tables, all with a distant musak lingering in the background. One other ageing gentleman sat blankly opposite me; before us, swam back and forth, the thin tidal wash of more blank-faced shoppers interspersed with grim store assistants and I suddenly held this image of being in the waiting-room to the valley of lost souls, expecting the grim reaper to appear at any moment and call out the next number. In that moment, the space held such a suspended air of timeless separation from the rest of the world - somewhat like a still from a Fritz Lang movie. And I realise in this moment, that I am seeking to record moments in time which are forever gone and which will never come again ... and which will, in all probability, be totally alien to those who might someday read them.

There comes a time, when one becomes tangibly-aware of the limits of one's mortality and wonders, 'What was that really all about ... What was the point?' ... and so, here I sit down to seek the point and to write something like this - not to proclaim myself to the world remaining in my inevitable absence; not to indulge in some narcissistic effort to leave a final imprint; rather, to seek some reason, for my own peace of mind, by retreading these conscious remnants of moments which once seemed so real and now, whilst still appearing to be so very tangible, are no longer here ... Poof! Gone! ... and one wonders whether all of it was (as has been wondered by countless others, before myself and wiser than I), just a thought - nothing more than, a dream.

* * * * *

IT AMAZES ME SOMETIMES, the things a person can manage to remember after so many years: the near and far details, events, sensations and atmospheres, the very soul of some moments - even down to the smells, which often provide a powerful catalyst for other remembrances ... and so often ... so very often, it feels like it took place only yesterday.

I'm not sure how far back our developed memory is supposed to consciously extend but I do seem to clearly recall tangible snippets from very early times - and I often find them so terribly-clear in all aspects of the senses, that I am certain they are not imaginings simply garnered from familial anecdotal sources.

I was to be the first child, having attended my parent's wedding in utero, and would be the only boy in a brood of four siblings. My parents had met while acting as part-time instructors in ballroom dancing at Sandy Robinson's Dance Studio in Brisbane, late in the 1940's; by late 1946, their carelessness had cemented my existence and, fortunately for us all, their love affair extended faithfully through the many ensuing decades. For fifty years, they bore their personally-perceived shame of my ex-wedlock conception before apologetically and quietly, revealing their 'terrible secret' to me as we celebrated their golden anniversary ... I, in my turn at that time, reassured them that I had gently and fondly borne that knowledge, since realising that simple mathematical fact from around the age of fifteen: at which time, I had rejoiced in the fact that I was a child of love.

For three years and nine months, the world was mine alone and I bathed in the loving light of my mother, whose luminescence was regularly further enhanced by that flowing from her own mother in the always-company of my mother's elder sister; these more evident than any other presences in that early world – even that of my father who by all accounts, did share in the joy of my being. Even later, with the arrival of number one sister, I did not feel particularly ousted; though there were sometimes, the to-be-expected look-at-me moments thrown in when I felt a waning of attention ... these displays were however, gently passed over with indulgent good humour, without pandering to their demands and I learnt quickly that I was not the sole occupant of the then-known universe.

We lived at two addresses during those early years. For my first two years, we occupied a small rear flat on the first floor of that grand, historic block of terrace houses on Brisbane's Coronation Drive; in those days, simply-named, 'Home Flats'. After that time, we resided for the next five years, halfway up the rising Tenneriffe end of New Farm's Villiers Street, close to the original power station. My father by that stage, having completed his apprenticeships with the tramways, had gained a responsible position as chief electrician to that generating facility. Now, sixty years later, its shell remains, converted in its final days to a lively arts centre, with performance spaces and trendy eateries fronting the river bank. The boiler rooms, control rooms and workshops have long been silenced and emptied ... and in their place, new occupants fill the air with the resonant sound of performance artists in its vaulted bowels and the din of enthusiastic diners on its perimeters, with the attendant roar of social discourse which now fills such spaces after dark.

I continue to vividly recall the arrangement of both of these homes. I remember details from 'Home Flats' – the progression of rooms in that extended residential finger sticking out into the terraces' rear courtyard spaces; leading from bedroom and basic bathroom through to the live-in kitchen at the furthest end, with our open verandah alongside; of my entertainment in a wooden-dowelled playpen out on that verandah, tossing my toys down into the bowels of the lower level courtyard, all for the simple pleasure of watching Mum fetch and return them – only to have me repeat the process for my own amusement; of my sitting, solitary and unattended, on the kitchen floor with cupboards open while I 'cooked' for Mum ... breaking eggs into a mound of flour and cereal emptied onto the floor in front of me; and most tangibly, of being naked under the green floral eiderdown on my parents' bed, relishing the delicious feel of the smooth satin's coolness against my skin, this moment possibly forming the genesis of a lifetime's love of sensual pleasure. Anecdotal sources alone could never account for such a strong memory of a purely-tactile sensation.

The house at New Farm in its turn, provides an even greater wealth of memories of all kinds. These stretch from my age of two-plus-something, until into my seventh year. I could draw the plan of that house now (not just a house but truly home through these years, where the front verandah with its timber-slatted blinds constantly collects a layer of black grit, deposited from the nearby power station – a fate often suffered by washing hanging on the line also) and clearly visible in my memory, is the lasting image of where I sat in that house (the very details of the bulky faux leather and tapestry sofa itself) on my mother's knee, as she introduced me to my first books: a popup, seen-through-the-cutout-layers version of Kingsley's 'The Water Babies' appears specifically in that particular image. Again, I vividly recall the cut, colour and tactility of the fabrics of so many of the clothes which my mother made for me in those earliest years: one shirt and a little pale-blue self-figured silken tie in particular; and here again, the experience of accompanying Mum with my baby sister in pram, down our hill and up the other slow side to the doctor's ... Janis has been discovered idly amusing herself in her cot, by plucking out kapok from a hole in the tiny mattress and shoving it up, just one nostril, until she can cram no more in. Even in this experience, I can still recall the feel of the waiting area at the doctor's surgery: a long, closed-in verandah space with casement windows down one side. Most doctors maintain their own singular practices in these years, with little more staff other than a multi-talented receptionist ... and so, most of them remain for a very long time afterwards.

My small family wait outside the entry walkway along one side of the little brick Methodist church, on the day of Jan's christening – Mum, Dad, along with my aunt and godmother, Mum's sister, Norma. It is only a small vignette of a remembered moment but strong and clear.

I continue to see an image of the lightweight (probably demountable), low-set early-years classroom block on the lower slopes of the primary school grounds in New Farm, where I am first enrolled in preparatory class ... of sleep periods in the afternoon, during one of which, the little girl beside me and myself find ourselves being gently chastised for quietly arguing as to who has the biggest willy ... of when I am soundly-ridiculed by the teacher (I am no more than five, mind you), for referring to a cow as a 'moo-cow'. Later in time, there exist other recollections of when I enter the first grade; of the dim, low and cavernous, cloistered brick undercroft of the main building – where wooden bench seats span between the rows of low, arched pillars and where we gather, run and play during the rainy days; of that one day when my scalp is injured by a remnant bolt-stub projecting from the playground's retaining wall, after a team of older boys in pursuit of a football, pile in their group tackle onto me as I unwittingly play marbles in the shadow of this wall, forcing me against the steel stub.

Here looms the haunted house set back and rising up above its yard, where we fearfully pass by it every afternoon, carefully-crossing to the other side of the road, as our small group makes its way home from school ... the front garden grows long and unkempt in a sea of waving paspalum, while a rocking chair sitting at the top of the front stairs holds a nest of pale grey cushions – very convincingly reading to our young eyes, as the sun-bleached skulls of careless schoolboys gone before. It is a long walk for a very small boy, along the heights at the back of Teneriffe, from our school to home back in Villiers Street. Even with only a couple of child companions and in the absence of any adults, all young children could do it and did. It represents the difference, the then relative innocence, of our world as it presented itself.

We have good neighbours here, though I do remember only our most immediate neighbours and they, are destined to remain good friends with our family long after we have left this neighbourhood. On the high side of the house, we have the Cripps family who seem to have had no children of their own, so far as my own memory serves. On the lower side of us, lives the Houlihan household and they do have considerably-older children still living at home. Theirs is the only home which I remember ever entering and even now, the image remains with me, of their large open dining area in back where we on occasion, shared a meal with them. We seem to enjoy a closer relationship with them, for I remain conscious of regular friendly exchanges there. Their dining room holds a brick fireplace whose chimney can be seen from our yard, poking up through the roof; and they take mild humour in correcting my childlike reference to their 'chimbly' ... and to the 'punkins' which they grow in the back of their property. Down in the hollow at the bottom of our hill, we are close to another couple who remain for a very long time, close and dear friends: Amy and Bob – the Gosleys. They are similar in age to Mum and Dad but at this time, childless; though I do recall from my parents' talk, that they did eventually have a child. They own a cute little two-seater, open-top sporty vehicle which memory claims as being an Austin. We do spend a lot of social time with them and they are always good company to be with.

My mild and gentle paternal grandfather, Bert and Dad squat on our back stairs one idyllic summer's afternoon, as they patiently and slowly turn the handle of the timber-slatted ice-cream churn to prepare an iced treat by hand. Inside, there is an intermediate stainless-steel sleeve containing crushed ice and salt as the freezing mixture, which then surrounds the core of vanilla custard being slowly turned by the churn itself. In the background, our chooks roam the lower yard and the baby kangaroo sleeps for a summer or two under the house in the makeshift pouch of a hung-up sugar bag. This Joey's mother had previously, been unwittingly despatched by the earlier-mentioned uncle on one of his regular spotlighting ventures with his ex-army mates – a long time before his rheumy eyes set in. This young kangaroo grows under our care, spars playfully with Dad in the long afternoons and, when he finally grows too big to be contained by our suburban backyard, he is placed in the care of family friends who have a soft heart and abundant space on their farming property.

Christmas mornings, I awake at daybreak to find an old pillowcase overflowing with gifts hanging from my bedpost. This is then excitedly-dragged next door and onto The Parents' bed, waking them at this ungodly pre-dawn hour and there, opened gift by gift under their sleepy but joyful eyes. This annual ritual, soon to be shared with my new sister, persists long through early childhood and beyond – and into yet another future address.

In this home, there sits in back, a mostly-unused spare room, lodged between the children's bedroom and the kitchen. Here, with its towering wall of large open-storage pigeonholes, stashed-away tea-chests of unused items, cartons, tools and other anonymous containers, this abandoned room is lit by one single bare bulb hanging from the ceiling, making it the very scariest place to be sent to fetch things from, after dark ... and then, there are always, The Dreams ....

* * * * *

THERE ARE RECURRENT DREAMS in these times ... in this house – not dreams as such but rather, certain half-waking visions which repeatedly come in that dim twilight region lying over the slow slide from wakefulness to sleep; if consciously focussed on, they will abruptly evaporate. My bedroom (later to be shared with my new sister) lies halfway down the central hallway with one single window,

MY FATHER'S GHOST: A MEMOIR

outside of which and somewhat elevated above it, is the bare expanse of the Cripps' gravel driveway. Here in my limbo each night, I travel one or another of these strange, purely-visual paths – repeatedly, without fail ....

I move through a tall and narrow streetscape hemmed-in by three or four storied residential buildings of plainly-Mediterranean appearance but in their entirety, constructed of smooth, orange-red, unglazed terracotta. Everything is made from this terracotta: the roadway, the cars, pets, the people themselves – like a giant personal diorama. Suddenly, travelling at speed from around one corner comes a locomotive, clearly of the same, baked-clay composition, which proceeds to crash into and demolish everything which stands in its path! This is all too much and a level of consciousness returns for the moment.

Again, I walk a long, long jetty of sunbaked, silvered and weathered planks over an expanse of deep, still water and the jetty leads to a distant bank – almost. One-by-one, sections of decking peter-out, progressively, until there remains only the tenuous line of a single plank and after that, the free-standing wooden piles only – and then, nothing. The safety of the far bank remains excruciatingly beyond reach. Turning and looking-back the way I have come, I now find that the return route suddenly looks the desolate same as the way forward and there is nowhere left for me to go ... and still, the relentless sun beats down from a clear blue sky. Lost in panic once more, I return to seek refuge in the conscious world still held within the covers of my bed.

On another occasion, I find myself standing on the grassy verge of yet again, a river bank, where the ground beneath me commences to crumble away and slip down into the depths of the water. I leap to the safety of solid ground, only to discover that also, crumbling away in the same loose fashion and however much I leap to safety ... again the seemingly-safe bank parts company with solid ground and once more slips away. These are the points at which fear pulls me back to the ready safety of consciousness.

I now have entered a claustrophobic, rectangular crawlspace which is contained by cold and dark, damp and glistening, roughly-cut stone surfaces. I must have started at the school by now, for the point of entry to this tunnel seems to be associated somewhere within my New Farm school. I finally come to the end of the shaft and find myself looking outwards and downwards from a highpoint opening in a similarly-wet stonewall looming above my own house, with no way down and retreat impossible, so tight is the fit.

These visions do not all confront me in each and every fall into sleep but they recur on a regular basis, often in twos or threes, following on each other. Finally, there is the most abstract and elusive of all these recurring, not-dream, image sequences from these years ... I hold between my thumb and first two fingers a small, nebulous spherical object; there is a feeling of fluctuating light and of a tremendous, spinning energy contained within it ... almost like the entire power of a universe being held in microcosm. There accompanies it, an overwhelming sensation of being sucked into it forever but in the very moment when I try to focus my attention in order to identify its reality, the image promptly dissolves. This particular 'dream' experience is one (and the only one) which is destined to repeat itself at further intervals throughout my life, even into parts of early adulthood during the odd waking moment, where the accompanying sensation of being drawn-in becomes increasingly disturbing. This has always remained an intriguing enigma, almost forgotten now ... but never, quite.

There would be other dreams of course – we all have them, even if most pass unremembered ... but none of such an exact, recurring content and not lodged in that twilight period hovering between wakefulness and sleep. In the high school years, there will be a recurring dream of flying – which I gather, is quite a common experience. In mine, I am always floating above the school oval at State High; not so much flying, as wearing seven-league boots. I take one springing step which carries me into the air, higher and higher, to perform extended leaps way over the top of power lines in graceful, flying strides as far as I choose to go ... then, to descend and in another step to be airborne again. It is wonderful and the more so, for being in such control of it. These are the most memorable later dreams but for one, which is to impact upon me in London one night many years later. But that is another story, best left until then.

* * * * *

LIFE HERE, IN THIS sometimes soot-gathering house, during these very early years contained on balance, little other than good memories. Dad's workmates busied themselves in the power-station workshop prior to every Christmas, spending all their spare moments crafting simple but colourfully-wonderful toys to be handed out to their own and others' children at their festive season's family party. Travel was by public transport or foot ... New Farm Park with its jacarandas provided a glorious route to the ferry terminal and thence, across river to make our way to grandmother's house. Time passed slowly, comfortably and securely. My sister and I entertained ourselves with our own imaginations and curiosities, always content in our own company. Our neighbours were warm, congenial and considerate, remaining as family friends long after we had moved on from New Farm.

Eventually, life and our location would change. A large, modern power station has been built at Tennyson, on Brisbane's south-side and our white-overalled father is transferred, to be elevated there into the role of electrical foreman ... he is to be their Mister Fixit, most times on-call at any hour for repairs to whichever piece of equipment might be broken down on the electrical-generating side of things. These call-outs hold nothing new for us and the main change to our lives as a family is a change of address: a different home in a different part of town at Yeronga, close to the power station and with different neighbours and a different school at Yeronga Primary ... and somewhere around this first year's turning, we gain yet another sister: Glenys, who will eventually be a middle child, bearing with her all the burden which that status reputedly brings in terms of family psychologies.

Home Flats, Brisbane's Coronation Drive, 1947. Originally built as Cook Terrace in 1888-1890

With Mum & Dad, September 1947, Given Terrace

MY FATHER'S GHOST: A MEMOIR

Villiers Street, New Farm, circa 1952

With Jan at the Gosley's, in Villier Street, circa 1954

My Grandparents, Herbert & Elizabeth Drew, approximately 50 years earlier, circa 1916.
Conte crayon & compressed charcoal on cartridge paper: my later drawings.

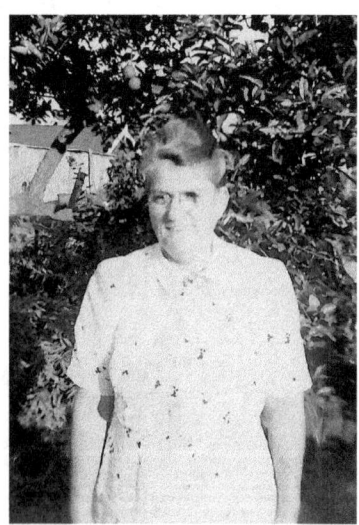

Herbert & Elizabeth Drew, c. 1945, at Fernberg Road, Rosalie; soon approaching my time.

MY FATHER'S GHOST: A MEMOIR

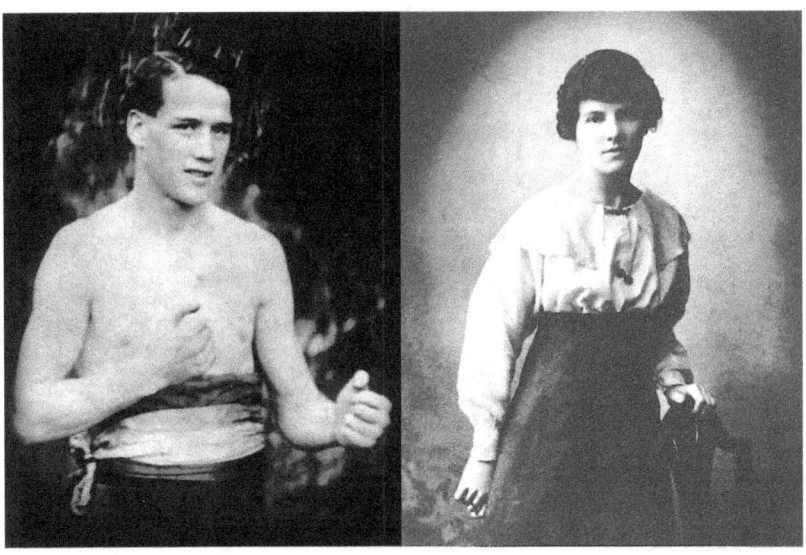

My other Grandparents, Albert Locke (Featherweight champion) & Emma Lavina Ashby.
In their youth prior to marriage, circa 1920, Brisbane.

With Mum & Dad, the first of many Currumbin holidays, circa 1948.

MY FATHER'S GHOST: A MEMOIR

With Jan, at Currumbin, circa 1953

Dad at New Farm Park, circa 1949.

Mum & Dad, Wedding, December 1946

2

Yeronga: and A New Home

THE YEARS AT YERONGA contain vast tracts of blankness, or at best, a vagueness like some half-remembered, precious memento which became lost in one of the bottom drawers of life's memory. However, in the spirit of this memoir I seize upon those elements which survive, disjointed as they may appear, in an effort to discover the underpainting residing underneath that final, somewhat-smudged and blurred portrait.

Having spent fifteen formative years there, every detail of the Eversley Terrace house, right down to the last idly-torn strips of wallpaper hanging forlornly from the wall above one sister's bed in the room she shares with the other sister, is indelibly imprinted on my life's page and with it, an almost unbroken newsreel of our life there ... but little of those very-first days at the infants school where I have now entered into the second grade. This is in the lower-school area which is housed separately from the upper grades, on the far lower side of the headmaster's residence and tight within its own fenced enclosure. I imagine the thought was that those very-young children have a tendency to wander and so need confinement in a more-limited space. Any other recollection of life in second grade fails to register in any part of my long-term memory. Entering third grade is when one graduates to the upper school and I can retrieve very little by way of any other memories of that initial year. Most primary school details after this are at best, sketchy and many names are lost now, back in the dim dank vaults of childhood ... a few sparse pieces do survive, if only under a thick layer of dust and with the certain mustiness of a long-neglected cellar, where old bottles of wine acquire an inflated value, often lacking in their youth ....

There is a tall, lean girl in these first years, taller than most of us, with long, dark, ponytailed hair and bearing the name of Jacqui McIntyre ... I secretly admire her in a held-in-awe sort of way. A screening clinic in a large van visits the school, weeding-out victims of TB ... and overnight, she vanishes to whatever fate awaits her with the dreaded consumption. She is never seen at this school again, nor heard of again in my own life and yet she left, for whatever reason, a strong imprint, right down to her name.

Here, in third grade, there enters a rather senior, and bluntly-fearsome, lady teacher whose name once stayed within my reach for a very-long time but even that has now fled into the mist (in retrospect, I suspect she was at core, a kindly teacher but there was then, to my young and uncertain naivete, an overbearing matriarchal presence to her). Here I am placed in the back row of class, being considered bright and of good behaviour – and here, I sit alongside one lovely Margaret West (who will return at intervals through later stages in my life). Margaret takes great pleasure in pinching and tickling me to such a degree that I squirm about in discomfort and I am promptly demoted as the culprit, down to the front row ... Oh! The injustice of it! Nevertheless Margaret and I do remain friends right through those early years. Books have always been favourite companions for me from the earliest of days and a few years later, probably around fifth grade, we find Margaret devouring a never-ending series of light, 'girls'-own' style of novellas, which she then passes on to myself ... I who will read most-anything offered. In contrast to the 'dragon-lady' teacher of year three, year four or five sees my first crush arrive: a young woman teacher, attractive both in looks and manner ... a Miss Young or some such name ... young or old, lady teachers were all Misses in those times – not a 'Mrs' nor a 'Ms' to be encountered anywhere.

Very little else from the early days of these particular school years stands out ... barring one instance of receiving a caning for fighting on parade – and it is not so much as for our concerted wrestling on the ground, the two of us, but for the fact that I happen to lash out at the teacher who tries to separate us, believing him to be yet another student joining-in ... we are probably not much more than fourth graders. So it is promptly, off to The Office for a 'Hands out, palms up, boy', by our headmaster, 'Sticky' Stevens. His unfortunate nickname is derived jointly from the cane he always carries and leans on, along with his lean and gaunt stick-insect appearance. He is severely bent-over prematurely, by what now I feel sure, is due to an advanced state of ankylosing spondylitis: an affliction I know, as I am later to discover as a young adult, as it affects my own body – though not ultimately, with the same 'bamboo-back' degree of deformation which is a trademark of the disease. I do hold more sympathy for him now, with this knowledge, than I held fear of him then.

Images remain with me of lining up every morning teatime for our mandatory half-bottle of milk which is by that time, moving far beyond tepid as it sits in its shallow crate, awaiting us out in the full morning sun. There I have one good friend, David Mackeral whose father is a school teacher someplace else – he is a good type, of sound background, but David also fades into the mists of time with the end of primary school and for some inexplicable reason, I continue to carry this consciously-unfounded thought that he eventually becomes an engineer; and yet there is another good friend in these fleeting times, Brian Rodwell, who one year gives me a wonderful 'Treasury of Science' book for my birthday ... his family are Bahai and one day, he has to bring a pneumatic donut cushion to sit on in school due to a boil in his nether regions and he makes such a terrible mess of cutting his own hair one weekend, he comes to school on Monday looking like a badly-tufted rug – and there exists in his family, a lovely, much-older sister, Helen ... for whatever unknown reason, I will always remember him and his family strongly and affectionately.

Finally, there is yet one other, be it skinny and weedy friend, John Shield, who also has a lovely older sister, Estelle ... John's main claim to fame in these closing years of primary school, is his absolute love of Elvis Presley and he performs (very loudly but very convincingly, in his raw young voice) jerky, knee-trembling, air-guitar impersonations of Elvis The Pelvis, whilst being urged on by our other classmates, down in the lower schoolyard during lunch-breaks. Around about this time, a cricket ball from out of nowhere fells me as I walk by the edge of the oval during our lunch break ... an innocent and unsuspecting bystander, caught between slips. I personally, never manage to feel any attraction for sporting activities during all of my school years, as I much prefer my books and music, my constant companions and distractions – even today, I hold very little interest in most sporting activities, especially those hysteria-infused team sports which appear to now be the lynchpin of our culture. Finally, in these last years on the eve of the transition to high school, comes a teacher who leaves a strong mentoring impression on me: one Trevor Howland – a tall, truly-manly mentoring example, stern but always-kindly and interested in developing the academic in the child ... a fine teacher in all respects, including that of respect, both given and received.

* * * * *

RUNNING PARALLEL with these early school years (which seem to stretch out forever like some vast canvas where each brushstroke is laid down in miniature and with infinite patience), is the life at our new home in Eversley Terrace, where we all grow and multiply with the same slow motion footage, to make our way into and through yet-another lifetime sequence. Once again, assorted bundles of recollections tumble out of the archives with a mostly-random patterning. There is initially, only myself in the company of one sister to occupy our mother and I can see her at the old Singer treadle sewing machine, happily producing clothes not just for the two of us but also, along with miniature versions for our collection of dolls. I do have my own boyhood toys but I also share dolls with my little sister (after seventy-odd years, I still have my now-politically-incorrect, but then and now still-wonderful, colourful, friendly, handsome felted golliwog stored safely away ... he has managed to survive the ravages of time, one inundating flood and unkind feasting by countless moths at various times) and on rainy days, we drape blankets over garnered chairs, gathered on our weathertight verandah, in order to create caves and huts where we happily play and amuse ourselves. On such days, I take my hoard of paddle-pop sticks and with them, embedded and plastered with mud, create dams across the many trickling small ravines which carve their way, as runoff from the front yard, down through the low confined spaces nestling under our home. Returning from school on rainy days, we remove our shoes in order to ski down the mossy channels of the gutters flanking the higher sloping sections of our street. School is probably the best part of two or three kilometres away, across the railway station footbridge ... and we walk there and back every day, with and then later without, Mum who never ever learnt to drive. Here at Yeronga, as was at New Farm, we always walk to school. Later, with the advent of our move to high school, set at a much greater distance some suburbs away, it will be public transport followed by a shorter walk from bus stop to school.

To one side of us, live the Russ family, who always wanted a girl but after three sons, have abandoned the idea. On the other, slightly-higher side of our property, live the Smiths with the only brick house within any sort of proximity, and a high-set at that. Earle has always wanted a son but after four girls grace the family with their presence, he eventually accepts that it is not meant to be. Here, in between, lodges our own family of a son and a daughter, eventually swelling to two, then three daughters. The son plays with the boys next door, building cubby houses and a series of increasingly-serious go-carts which hurtle down our raw, unsurfaced side driveway, one eventually towing a trailer in tandem behind it. They all play on the littered slopes of the local refuse dump, sliding down its ramparts on sleds formed from sheets of rusty iron or of heavy cardboard, collecting all manner of real treasures, from old carbide headlamps and bunsen burners, to discarded surveyors' tripods and a large stash of imperfect electric razors dumped from the Sunbeam factory up the road – these, the eldest next-door son proceeds to clean and restore to working-order, which he then shares with every male of shaving status that he knows, including my own father who then continues to shave resolutely with his, well into his latter years.

The girl, unsurprisingly, plays with the growing bevy of girls next door; on occasion, siding with them to launch surprise missile attacks on the son. At these times, he is caught in a barrage of rotting mangos – the annual excess from our own very-prolific tree, which graces us with a cornucopia of fruit throughout most summers: stringy, turpentine monsters which we messily-eat, or peel and squeeze into juice for drinking just-so, or to be frozen in metal trays as ice-blocks. Both neighbours each harbour one child older than this singular son and secretly, he admires the elder of the girl brood, Margaret, never daring to openly admit the fact. Much later, when they are both attending university, she will often ferry him there in her tiny green Morris. Nothing more is ever to transpire ... her first-arrived sister, on the other hand, will one day ask him to accompany her to the senior school formal after which, as he very-properly escorts her back home, she will take him by surprise by suddenly wrapping him in a passionate embrace at the threshold to their kitchen door. He flees like a startled hare, clearing their not-so-very-high common fence-line in one long-legged, green and gormless leveret bound – a reaction which he might quite possibly replay and so, greatly confound his late night thoughts in later years.

Dad keeps a collection of ducks – muscovy and khaki-Campbells mostly, with the odd Indian runner ... for all of whom, he holds a great fondness: they make good pets, while Mum uses their eggs in everything she cooks, making for the very-best cakes including the lightest, float-away sponges and, on those very special occasions throughout the year, when others are eating chicken or turkey, we are dining on delicious roast duck with little or no guilt – the most special of our pets always manage somehow, to escape this occasional annual culling. Mum also makes the old-fashioned, giant globes of suet-enhanced Christmas puddings in calico cloths, which then hang for weeks in the open-air under the kitchen sink, gathering traces of mould and waiting to be reheated and gently peeled of their cloths at Christmas time – the inclusion of old-fashioned suet provides a delicious dense, glazed texture which lifts them way above any other dried-fruit-based puddings ever known to man. Throughout our year, we regularly dine on various forms of offal (for economy's sake in reality), which are so well-presented by our resourceful mother, that we always regard them as treats and luxuries ... brains, hearts, livers, kidneys, tripe (the lungs, much prized for their inclusion by the Scots in their haggis, are the only parts that escape our mother's stovetop) – even our beloved ducks have their complete offal offerings, including lower-wings and feet much-prized by our father for their gelatinous quality, turned into the most delicious soup, over which we vie for the various parts. Our father also maintains a small vegetable garden with varying degrees of success, growing silverbeet, spring onions, carrots and beans ... and he regularly maintains his own car, accompanied by the occasional gentle expletive whenever a spanner slips, rasping his knuckles – everything from changing the oil to honing the cups on the valve pistons. At the power station, he is Mr Fix-everything-that-breaks-down and at home, he is also Mr Fix-and-mend-everything ... his versatility and practicality know no bounds.

His payoff for all this dedication at home is his revered Lodge. He rehearses his secret Masonic practices in our front sunroom, doors closed and alone or with his friend, 'Rollo' Wiles, from the hill across the way from us. Then, they follow up with their official practice nights, which are followed by the real thing ...when they set off in their immaculate dinner suits, carrying their regalia cases in hand, looking for all the world like American mobsters with gun-cases tucked under their arms. Over the years we glimpse numbers of them, queued like rookeries of penguins, at bus ranks on dusk and we instantly-know where these 'not-really-gangsters' are going with their little black cases clutched under their shiny black wings.

Dad takes this all very seriously and over the years, rises through the ranks to the honourable stature of the Grand Poobah Beelzebub-something, or whatever they might actually call him (if you will forgive my bemused cynicism), for a season after which, he is a Past Master of something 'terribly secret' (and here I am reminded for some reason or other of my beloved Famous Five – God only knows why). These regular evening absences on his part, help to further the bond between the young boy and his mother ... for it is their own treat night. Late afternoon, I scale the back-fence-but-one from ours, to trade comic books with the yet-another all-boy family who live there, who in their turn, harbour a rich library of such literary pulp-fiction and other masterpieces, all hoarded away in a single, big, old-fashioned tea-chest, absolutely overflowing with them – which is a grand lot of comic books. Mum has some soft drink set aside for us (a treat in itself in these times) and either sweets or small packets of crisps and with them, we retire to my parents' bed to prop ourselves up against the pillows and each read our own debatably-intellectual literature (mine admittedly, not so highbrow as hers), whilst we indulge ourselves in our contraband treats, until Dad returns home. It is his 'boys club', but nevertheless, a seriously-taken one and while they may have had on hand, some beer at supper afterwards, I never knew Dad to have any himself at those times.

Ours, during these years, is essentially a mildly-Methodist family ... it remains non-wowser – balanced, low-key and far from extreme in any moralistic view of the world. We attend church and Sunday School and Mum sings in the choir, as later, so do I – firstly, in the junior choir and then later, also in the senior choir. I enjoy the singing but the rest of it really, remains truly and simply, a matter of rote. I mutely accept the process without too much extended inner thought or consciousness ... neither, as I suspect, did very many of my companions of similar age in that then, peer group. As I grow older, moving into my early and then, mid-teens, I manage to glean my first girlfriends from this close social set – they are quite-possibly little-more conscious of any deeper meaning to this churchgoing than I am ... we simply follow in our parents' own obedient footsteps and it is, for that contained time, the only social group we know. In later years, at university, I am to fully acknowledge this dissociation for what it is, at which time I feel impelled to formally cut my ties with it. In the meantime, we Yeronga-raised Methodists are not by any means, such absolute wowsers: we dance at all of Dad's Lodge socials and for Christmas lunch at his mother's, we are even allowed a small nip of sherry (mine mixed with cold lemonade, for the greater sensibility's sake).

* * * * *

DAD'S MOTHER, my so-very-matriarchal grandmother, tends to be just that – Grand and Matriarchal. My Mum's own mother by contrast, is gentle, loving and low-key. She was an Emma Lavinia Ashby before marriage to my grandfather, Albert Locke. Emma Lavinia is purportedly at this time, placed somewhere on the short line of descent from a certain Lord Ashby, of Ashby de la Zouche, in Leicestershire, England, about whom there floated through the family during my teenage years, a mythology surrounding the Lord's then-recent death and the matter of a missing will, reputed to be destroyed by his second wife, greatly-piqued (understandably for her) on discovering the scant provisions made for her future in that document ... and were we mentioned therein? Nothing more is ever again heard of that matter – in all likelihood, it exists as no more than the wishful conjecture by members of a struggling post-war family in that fantasised moment, falling into the realms of family mythology and very little more. It does seem that the estate and the castle do fall into the hands of the state in the very-real absence of a will ... and there, the castle languishes and eventually falls into ruin.

This very-dear, maternal grandmother and her family maintain a dominant presence through all my early childhood years and well-into my teens. They live in a modest weatherboard house on timber stumps at Kangaroo Point, with a frontage to Baines Street and a backyard which empties into Raymond Park, an elongated patch of green, devoid of much in the way of trees, which serves the local community as a sports field and training ground in the afternoons and weekends, occasionally resounding to cheers and hurrahs from a smattering of enthusiastic supporters. On Saturday afternoons, these sounds are accompanied by the mechanical, rattling, cicada-like chorus of manual push mowers being plied through every other of these back yards – all as a backdrop to the harsh serenade of horse races being called out from a matching myriad of portable radios. The homes are all similar, timber, high-set, pre-war houses, cheek to jowl in tidy lines down the street; this one opens from on high, onto a car mechanic's yard down along one of its sides. Each day, horse-drawn-mostly, carriers deliver vegetables; or crusty and light, almost-still-steaming, hot fresh bread and buns; or bottles of fresh milk topped with an inch of thick cream and closed off with foil caps; or else, early each morning, large blocks of ice are delivered, to be rushed into the house, held within large metal tongs and there, dropped into the waiting tops of the many iceboxes which are still in use in most households here.

A fly-screened meat safe hangs from the rafters of the back verandah while hot water is boiled in the drum of gas heaters, lit by matches and sitting over the ends of the bath or over the kitchen sink.

My grandmother, Emmy, cooks on a very large wood stove, which is responsible for creating the most delicious roast dinners, while the best-ever toasted bread is browned on a long-handled fork held within the bowels of the cosy open firebox. This stove, sitting at one end of its own large kitchen, forms the ever-active hub of the household and the windows here, still have some upper panes covered over by the sheets of brown paper taped to them, which had served to black-out houses during the war years ... even now, in the distant wake of the war, they continue to provide a reminder to those who lived through those years of uncertainty. This is where the family happily gathers, night and day. The firewood is chopped every day, at the bottom of the backstairs, by Whopper the Woodchopper – he is my grandmother's almost-invisible brother ... I've never known his real name (but that it terminated with Ashby) nor can I recall what he ever looked like. The only memory of my Great-uncle Whopper is of a shy and damaged man who hid, for most of the time, in his room off the rear verandah between the kitchen and the remainder of the house, sleeping (if such, his nightmare-ridden life can have allowed him) much of that time. This sleep was regularly interrupted by cries from behind his closed door of, 'Oh! Oh! Ooooahh!!!' as he was chased by the large red bull, which waited for him daily behind the closing of his eyes. Even now, I can only surmise that he also, remained a tragic reminder of the war just passed. I have no memory of when or how he died. I was young and some things you don't notice ... or don't wish to.

My grandfather Albert is kindly, if prone to make late returns home after work, via a little socialising at his Pineapple Hotel, which is perhaps too conveniently close to home, being only at the end of the street. He might be gently admonished but nevertheless, my grandmother mostly tolerates this predictable occurrence and evenings are not truly marred by this ritual. He likes to fish and sometimes returns with a good catch of delicious jewfish or a sugar bag full of large, thrashing, live mud crabs which are to be cooked right then and there. He works by day as a compositor with a city newspaper, and smokes roll-your-own cigarettes, as many did and continued to do. At his end of days, this is to prove to be an unfortunate combination as, for when he does die, it is to be from bladder cancer - a common end for smokers working in his trade ... it is the lead - and by that, the continual carrying of it to the lips by the act of smoking ... the kiss of death, one might say.

In his youth, when he met my grandmother, he was a lean, good-looking amateur boxer - Super Bantamweight to be specific. There remains a posed photo of him amongst the sparse family papers still existing, bare chested and poised for action in his fighting sash and trunks, while the records of his fights - wins, draws and losses remain available in the boxing annals from that time. She herself, was a pretty, petite and demure young woman and it undoubtedly made for love at first sight.

There are two other residents at Baines Street: my mother's brothers - my uncles. Albert Arthur is the eldest son in a brood of five siblings - as a soldier, he spent a large part of the war stationed in New Guinea after which, as a cabinet-maker and carpenter, he established himself as a builder in the area around Cairns. The large Italian population in the north took him as one of their own, declaring he looked the part and renamed him simply as 'Joe' ... and so, he remained as Joe Locke until the end of his days ... with family and friends, forever, Joe. His, are the departed uncle's eyes which sometimes now, arise to confront me in my bathroom mirror. It was he, Joey, who went spotlighting from utilities with his army mates on weekends and provided the orphaned little joey, who would be nursed by my parents at New Farm.

Dudley Graham is the other uncle, the baby of the family, who is never to be known as Dudley, but always as Graham ... or, as an alternative, during those years of the fifties, is to be bridled with the known-by-close-family title of 'Bodge'. Being the youngest of that family, he is only ten years older than myself and so, through my early teenage years, provides something of an influence on my development. He has a portable gramophone with a small but selective collection of inspirational recordings – Elvis Presley, Johnny Ray, Dave Brubeck, Thelonious Monk, Miles Davis among others ... and Stan Freberg, my first taste of satire. He also, is a fan of the Goon Show and has a hidden treasure trove of Playboy magazines. Although he is my uncle, he is young enough to be my big brother. As a child, he experienced a period where he suffered with polio. As a result, he bears a wizened left arm and has a compromised heart valve. In defiance of the diminished arm, he goes on to become an excellent French polisher and because of the legacy of the heart, he later in life is to receive a pig's valve which saves his future for quite some number of years. Somewhere along the way, he has a brief fling with a girl from the far north and unknowingly, fathers a son who, many years later when he is a father himself, manages to track down his real father's family; only to find that he is too late ... his father is already dead! In the meantime, at a more or less mature age, our Uncle Graham successfully enjoys a happy marriage with a gentle Greek woman named Irene (which, as a small aside, means 'peace'), ten years his senior. Shortly, during this period of his life, his fortune changes when he wins $30,000 in the Golden Casket (a pittance now but significant then) and gains enough to purchase a news-agency in the inner suburb of Annerley, which he and Irene comfortably conduct until one day, years down the track, he meets a friend for a quick drink after work at their local and drops dead on his bar stool ... just like that! Until that moment, his life though a little compromised, had been charmed for a time and with such a swift ending, perhaps continued to be charmed.

This grandmother, Emma Lavinia, with her gentle personality, presents somewhat of a contrast with that of my other grandmother (Nana, as opposed to MaMa, the soft one) Elizabeth Price, formerly a Higgenson - a large family dating back via times in Ireland, to origins somewhere in Scandinavia, where they had been known as Øggrensen or something very similar. This is a strong family, full of strong personalities, including my sometimes-fearsome Nana, whose own mother bore fourteen children to my tall, stern-looking, robust and very ruggedly-Victorian great-grandfather, Robert Higgenson - a figure of grandeur if ever existed one. Although she emits something of this Victorian grandness, Nana is essentially soft at heart and is a kind, if at times matriarchal, woman who is to lose her loving husband Herbert, my gently-intelligent Papa, who survived two world wars only to abruptly drown one day before his time, without warning, in a flood of his own blood, from a suddenly, fully-ruptured aorta.

Papa Drew is not really a Drew. His own mother, with two children already in tow, had in her time, been suddenly widowed. With no means of support, she had been reduced to taking employment in a pineapple cannery to provide for herself and the children, my grandfather's half-siblings. Soon, she caught the eye of the manager of the factory (this is all starting to sound a little Dickensian - but it did happen) who made his move on the young mother and in a short time, she found herself very-seriously compromised, up-the-duff, pregnant. To add insult to injury, she then discovered that Mr Wonderful is not so very-wonderful ... he was already married with children of his own and she finds herself dropped like the proverbial hot-potato - not only that, she no longer has a job. At some point in this now-familiar melodrama, there entered a much-older man - single, of course. He offered marriage and security for her and the two children ... but not for the bastard - my grandfather. And so, Papa was fostered out to a local German family, named Kiel (after whom, a small mountain and a road became named in time, here in the Sunshine Coast hinterland). It is now 1915 and a war has arrived in Europe and the adopted son, though underage, goes to enlist. The recruiting officer advises my grandfather, Herbert Kiel, to modify his name to something not so-obviously German. He goes home to seek advice from his adopted mother who suggests he take her maiden name which, of course, is Drew. Herbert survives this war and returns home to then marry one Elizabeth Price Higgenson, then fails at being a successful pineapple farmer on his plot (which is the government's reward for surviving the great conflict) and follows up with more success as a baker, which is when his own children come into being. Not a large man by any means, he was an underage non-com private in one war and, as an older enlisted man, a cook in the next. I remember him with a large and gentle heart – which was suddenly no more … he was sixty-three, I was fourteen.

* * * * *

AT SOME EARLY STAGE (I forget my exact age), I am sent off to receive piano lessons from an elderly lady – short, plump and with thinning, fast-fading hair – who lives within walking distance from our home. Miss Davis lives alone. She keeps an old-fashioned wooden school ruler close at hand for correcting little fingers which might just play the wrong notes on the keyboard and she has a dog who seems almost as old as she is … perhaps it is. The dog is of moderate size and is firmly, tightly-rotund like a well-stuffed sausage – with scarce-little hair remaining, the odd whisker sprouting from its polished, grey, tightly-packed skin … and, like its mistress, it yaps.

These piano lessons, painful as they might be on fumbling occasions, are to be a longterm gift for me. I continue with them well into my high school years, by then, with a different teacher: a sweet, ageing, birdlike creature – a Miss Robertson, who sees me successfully complete fourth grade as an additional subject in my Junior year (now Grade 10) and indulges me in the interim and later, by permitting me to take on pieces which are far more advanced than I should really attempt. She allows this purely because I like them and desire to play them. I carry away from her, one of the best gifts of all: that of seeming in consequence, to be forever blessed with an innate ability for sight-reading music ... which sees me at one point in future time, after a twenty-odd year hiatus of the piano's total neglect, still being able to resume playing as if it had been only yesterday when I stopped.

This gift of piano tuition is to provide one of my life's mainstays, since from it grew a sound interest in and a great love of classical music, including grand opera. Perhaps also, because of my being blessed with an essentially eclectic nature regarding likes and loves in all of the arts, that love of music grew over time to embrace most other forms of music, from jazz to rock and beyond – even to the ethnic music of many other cultures ... and in all those varied forms, the music has attended and accompanied me always – as a looked-for background and constant companion to every life activity I have ever indulged in, particularly those interests pursued in solitude.

Dudley Graham, Papa, Norma, Mama, 'Joe', and new cousin Lesleigh.
At the farm, Central Lansdowne near Taree, circa 1961.

With Jan & Glenys, and with cousin Lesleigh, at Yeronga, circa 1960.

3

A Splendid Sequence of Summers

AND THEN, THERE ARE THE HOLIDAYS ... a fine annual family tradition emerges, which is to create the foundation for one of the strongest, most-tangible, lasting memories of childhood, stretching away forever into the future, where they will resonate with idealised clarity on every level of the senses ... Currumbin! Even today, thoughts of a desirable holiday location anywhere on our coastal margins are, in the main, coloured by the potency of those memories; as their recapturing becomes a more and more difficult task to satisfy, while the influx of holiday-making hordes from other states and profit-driven realestate agents compromise the finding of such idyllic venues for what was once such a simple holiday.

We first started vacationing at the Currumbin house-on-the-hill while I was still only a toddler, fresh on my mother's knee – probably coinciding with our earliest years in the New Farm house. That very-same, long-dead uncle from today's looking glass, Mother's big brother Joe, again enters the scene – for there is held in keeping for me, an image of my sitting on her knee up front in the cabin of his carpenter's work utility, while Dad sits braced against the cabin in the open back of it with our luggage, as we climb the hill to the rear entrance of 'Furlough'; it is night, the headlamps are on and for some reason, I always retained a strong image of that moment in particular. 'Furlough', halfway up the Currumbin hillside overlooking the wide expanse of that beach, would be our annual holiday destination, every Christmas season, for most of the next fifteen years. The house still lies today as it did then, across the hill and it is expansive in its outlook along its entire length but it is also cosy and safe in its sturdy containment; and that glorious sound, the thunder of the ocean is always present. There is a lower level, a secure undercroft which is reached by an internal flight of stairs ... it houses primarily the bathroom and little more: a large cube of a room, lined entirely in sheet galvanised steel – walls, floor and ceiling, which has developed a dark, warm patina over the years from its subjection to clouds of steam every day, since it is basically a terribly-large shower cubicle to luxuriate in, on one's way back up from the beach ... and that is all. Outside of it, there is a high, battened-in, enclosed area with a concrete floor where fishing rods are stored along with the smell of salt and sand; and where Dad and my uncles clean the eugarie, or pipi which they glean in a slow twisting dance along the wet shoreline as the wash of each wave recedes ... and which they then open, to use the oyster-like flesh as fishing bait. My slightly-younger cousin, Madeline, eagerly devours the eugarie meat as quickly as her father and Dad can open them ... it's a fierce battle for the bait between the maid and the anglers.

Upstairs, there is a sewered toilet cubicle attached at the back door (or is it the front door? ... as it is the only door into the house at that level) and there is a handbasin located in each of the bedrooms. One long, enclosed verandah runs in front of the bedrooms and opens to the ocean vista via a wide timber-slatted roller blind midway, where kookaburras come to be fed on the sill and this is where I sleep – the adults always have the bedrooms and the children have this giant sleep-out ... and it is good, being rocked to sleep by the lullaby of the surf. The kitchen is also out back of the house and fills with the aromas of lunchtime jaffles, toasted on the open burner on wet or lazy days and regularly, with that of fish ... fried fish, poached fish, grilled fish, fish patties, fish soup from the remnants of the carcasses, cooked with milk and onions and pepper ... no part of the ocean's treasure is wasted. When not cooking these indulgences hauled from the surf by the men, Mum can be found chopping finely the cheap seconds of mixed fruits from the local shop, which she then packs into metal trays and freezes into ice-blocks; long before the days of the packaged iced treats of Toowoomba's Les Weiss are first encountered.

There are one hundred and thirty-something concrete steps from the house, leading down the slope of this hill to the end of the lane which then feeds out onto the beach esplanade. On one side of the entry to the lane at the bottom of these steps, is a modest cottage to which the dean of my university faculty will one day retire. On entering the lane, the left side holds the bakery, wonderful with the smells of its fresh bread, above all else. It was from here, down these many raw concrete steps and from the immediate surroundings of the house itself, that some of the strongest memories remain: the olfactory ones. There was a smell ... that of sand (the house literally sat on sand, all that way up the hill) and of the sea, ozone, salt and the coastal banksias, pandanus palms, paperbarks and Norfolk pines ... which pervaded the air and shaped the clarity of my future ever-so-overpowering yearnings for a coastal environment.

There are isolated moments in time which seem to have stuck to the clinging constancy of memory ... I see us now, on towels against the rock wall below the esplanade – the season must have been cyclonic and the tides high. I am barely more than two years old, in knickers and a soft white cotton-brimmed hat. I remember that my grandfather (the doomed paternal one) is with us as a sudden rush of angry, agitated wave hurls itself up the beach, rushing for the rock wall and my father snatches me up, just in time, out of its grasp. There I am now, perched on Dad's shoulders, still little more than a skinny five, as he carries me in the deep, incoming tide back from Lion Rock to the rock-wall at the sand-works; and again, being borne high by him across a deep channel of the creek, Currumbin Creek, also adjacent to the old sand-works ... the sand-works are long-gone now, the creek mouth safely-redirected, the rock wall covered by a carpark and Lion Rock permanently-connected to the carpark by a wide spit of sand.

My father comes home from fishing off that rock wall, bearing a sugar-bag which contains the front half of a monster flathead, sheared-off halfway down its length by a shark, as he fought to land it ... all he felt was one sharp dull thump and suddenly, half of his catch was gone.

Early mornings, we walk around to the nearby bird-sanctuary where we feed honey and bread to the lorikeets from tin plates, pat the odd kangaroo and purchase the best fresh honey from the modest lean-to which constitutes their retail outlet and office ... today this is a major tourist attraction, grown out of all proportion and well-nigh impossible to gain a carpark nearby, except by chance.

My sister and I play on the rear garden steps behind the house, which lead up to the steeply-ascended back road: steps formed of concrete between walls of large rounded stones with cuppings of the ever-present sand, lodged in a similar stone wall. Down on the ground platform surrounding the house, sparse blades of grass grow through that sandy shelf and the sand's very smell pervades everywhere one walks. On rainy days and during storms, we hunker down in the snug, cupboard-lined, dining room to play simple card games or else read our books out on the verandah beds while the rain lashes the hillside. Even these days carry with them, a certain reassuring cosiness and comfort. At some point, we have gained a baby sister, who now shares our parents' room with her cot. Grandparents, uncles and aunts, along with our dear cousins, intermittently share this holiday space but it remains our very-own treasured annual refuge from the life of town – since Brisbane cannot truly be called a city yet and though some might think it so, it remains in essence, little more than a big country town.

Dad is never one to remain still for very long. So, on these seemingly endless holidays, we make outward excursions on an almost-preordained basis. We regularly make day trips to Murwillumbah, (where we always stop in at the Norco Butter Factory, there to be treated to delicious half bottles of flavoured milk) and thence, up to Binnaburra at Springbrook, and its Natural Arch (now, it seems for some politically-correct reason, to be renamed Natural Bridge) where my sister manages to be painfully stung by a native stinging bush; and then there are the return trips back down through Upper Currumbin and the Currumbin Valley ... these outings all involve precipitous drives around the edges of post-volcanic mountainsides in our old, soft-top Austin tourer on loose, unsealed roads where one side always seems to plunge down and away precipitously, too close to the passenger's seat for comfort, which causes enormous anxiety to my mother, who has no head for these things and the rattle of the wheels on loose gravel is often punctuated by distraught, increasingly-tremulous cries of 'Bill! Oh!...Bill!' Of less concern to her, are the visits to the lighthouses at Fingal Point and Byron Bay (which was then, still only a sleepy, distant surfing hamlet) and through the procession of small beachside towns linking them, south of the state border. None of these involve the scaling of mountainsides over winding dirt tracks in our old Austin tourer (not so old then, but undoubtedly a collector's item now) and our mother enjoys the journey without the accompaniment of cliffside terror.

There are other holidays of course, at other destinations, but none are to secure their place in our family's collective memory, quite like those of Currumbin.

There is at one time, a shared holiday with an aunt and uncle, along with our three cousins, which does call up strong images ... this is with the family of Dad's younger sister, Dorothy – that of cousin Madeline, the eugarie eater. It is a little further down time's track, as she now has twin siblings, Rodney and Susan and we have all travelled north to the lazy hamlet of Scarness. We share a low-set house together on the esplanade and the beach stretches away in a wide flat foreshore, almost as flat as the waters of the bay which gently wash it, and merges to become one with the bare expanse of narrow roadway which fronts it. As sometimes happens with twins, one of them, the boy, is healthy and strong whilst his sister is frail, weak and sadly, weak of mind – she is destined to live not far past the early years of childhood. She is pretty and loving in nature but fragile, delicately-diminished and simple. Her early and gentle death whilst tragic for all, will undoubtedly be a long-term blessing, for her at least. I can see her now, during the holiday, sitting on the sand of that foreshore, caught shovelling little spadefuls of it into her mouth; likewise, I see us five cousins, all feigning sleep during our mandatory rest periods in the afternoons; as I also see us discovering one morning, a litter of almost-countless baby sharks stranded on the beachfront as far as the eye might see. That beach front and its esplanade are now unrecognisable, while even the name has all but disappeared, as the busy retirement-township and whale-watching tourist destination of Hervey Bay has engulfed it with a trendy waterfront of eateries.

At yet another point in time, a different uncle, Tom along with our aunt, Norma (my mother's younger sister and my own godmother) make a major move south of the border, to redeem the running of the family dairy farm near Taree in Central Lansdowne, from his ageing father.

For several years after that, at the turning-over of my life into puberty, this becomes our summer holiday destination, accompanied by sisters one and two. Somewhere in this space on the farm, I am to gain yet another cousin, Lesleigh. The countryside here is mostly green and rolling, criss-crossed by gentle gullies, filling up the occasional farm dam and running off into small, tree-lined creeks which lead into the Manning River. In these lazy, idyllic surroundings, the novelty of life on a dairy farm makes for a host of fond memories, even if now randomly assembled. They rush in from every direction. Here resides Gussey, the only horse on the property – old and very spoilt, grown fat around the girth from a life of limited activity ... and a con-artist: catching and mounting him, involves making an approach down the paddock with corn kernels in one outstretched hand, bridle carefully-hidden in the other ... a con-artist if ever there was one. The bridle has to be slid quickly over his head and fastened around his neck before he finishes munching corn. The ancient, silver-planked barn houses a small mountain of corn ears at its heart, sitting behind the gaps in its planks, as the horse well-knows, and with a raw twelve- or thirteen-year old intent on riding him, this canny horse has him at his command ... once bridled and saddled, (he has a trick to play even in this, which consists of taking in a very-deep breath before the saddle straps are cinched – after which, his exhalation renders them loose and useless) he will not move anywhere under my urgings unless I first dismount and lead him down the yard, well-away from the barn ... then I can mount him and he will cheerfully return me back up the hill to the source of all corn-dom: the barn – there, to be bribed with a handful of corn kernels once more ... and so, I am his duped and gormless puppet.

There happens one year, when our summer household all drive to one of the neighbouring farms (this one holds a small orchard, as well as a pair of attractive daughters, somewhat older than myself) in order to harvest a couple of cases of small, barely-ripe peaches, which my aunt plans to preserve. The Vacola bottles sit in the pantry waiting at the ready, while the cases of fruit sit in the open laundry's tubs overnight. In the morning, the cases are empty and the ground all around is littered with the very-clean, spat-out peach pips, which are all that remains after our Gussey has glutinously feasted on them overnight.

The following year, in remembering these neighbouring young women, I saddle the horse and set off down the road to find them again. I have under-estimated the distance from home and before we can reach my goal, a mighty storm hits the horse and I, forcing me to seek shelter in a roadside milk-collection lean-to, with Gussey tethered outside of it. The return ride home, mounted on a wet saddle, proves to be an excruciating experience– standing in the stirrups or sitting on the saddle, makes no difference at all – my thighs are bruised and chaffed ... and, to add insult to injury, I am strongly upbraided on my return, since no one has known what I have done or where I have gone, save that the horse and I are gone and all have been worried for me. I never do manage to see those young women again.

I remember either riding Gussey or other times, driving my uncle's tractor (not a large one: a small blue Fordston Dexter), down to the lower paddocks to collect the cattle in for milking in the late afternoons; with which they happily comply ... mornings, they seem to know just when to get themselves up into the holding yard at the right time, without any external intervention. There they stand in the early morning light, nostrils steaming while the thin mud of the yard steams under them with the warmth of freshly-excreted urine. Then one morning, I find a new-born calf with her mother down in a gully and as I carry the calf gently in my arms back to the house, with mother lowing gently but trustingly-following along behind, the calf discharges its first motion – white, and sticky as pva glue, it mats itself solidly in the fine hairs of my thin pubescent arms.

The herd are individually named by my uncle, some of them more appropriately than others. There is one fondly-named after my grandmother Emma; there is of course, a little Audrey, after my mother ... and then there is another, who possesses a more than extremely-anxious disposition and she, he names Bebe, after yet-another aunt, my uncle's sister-in-law. They are all Jersey cows but this one is somewhat smaller and darker in colour with shadings towards black in parts. The rest of the herd amble quite-happily in their turn up from the steaming yard and into the milking bails. When her turn comes, this one skitters and clatters nervously across the concrete apron to the bail, all of the time with white, bulging eyes and panic-stricken looks thrown out from one side to the other. Once she is locked into the bail, with one leg firmly roped back, we await her inevitable discharge – a bucket ready in one hand, a sugar-bag to lay out behind her (in lieu of the shovel which is usually sufficient for the normal droppings of other cows) held in the other. From those early mornings and late afternoons, the atmosphere of the milking shed still rises up as if it were only yesterday: the smell of disinfectant bleach in the hot water used to clean down the equipment and to wash the udders; plucking gorged ticks (fat, purple, bloated monsters, to be swiftly-squashed underfoot) from their sides as they patiently await milking; the steady pulse of the milking machines and the slurp of the cups as they accept the proffered udders ... steam arising from the fresh urine in the muddied surface of the holding yard in early mornings and the warm squelch of it between the toes as the cattle are led in. There follows the pleasurable sensation of finger-feeding poddy-calves from buckets of fresh warm milk in order to wean them, at the rear of the milking shed.

And the vet who tends all these milkers, with his swollen lips purple from his Bex addiction which is to eventually kill him, dons his long-sleeved latex glove as he carries out artificial inseminations on the in-season cattle – the short-legged but pretty, little bull which my uncle innocently purchased, being unable to perform his husbandry duties without at least, the advantage of a stool to stand on ... Bex and Vincents powders were the household analgesic drugs of choice throughout the 1950s and 1960s; the advertising for them exhorted one to 'a cup of tea, a Bex and a good lie down' as the solution to everything from a simple bad day at the office to just about every complaint known – long-distance truck drivers took a cocktail of a Vincents in a small, old-fashioned bottle of Coca Cola as a pick-me-up solution to their fatigue ... these powders were effective and addictive, eventually destroying the kidneys. This is what finally happens to Bernie, the genial but doomed vet.

Ken Drury, a cheerful neighbouring dairy farmer and the deliverer of sermons at his local church once a week, demonstrates the power of music every Sunday evening, as he draws his milkers to their stalls, all lowing gently to the regional radio broadcast of church music and hymns which resounds loudly across the whole of the district. In another neighbour's direction over the hills, lies a farm where not one, but two bulls reside ... these frequently contrive to make their way into one or the other's holding yard. There then issues a chorus of frenzied beefing and bellowing across the neighbourhood, in a short while to be interrupted by the single boom or two of a saltpetre-packed shotgun cartridge blast – a final, loud single bellow is then swiftly followed by total silence, as they are brought to heel, calmed-down and once more, separated. Other than these happenings, life is quiet and relaxed ... perfect as an end-of-year holiday for all of us. My mother is with her probably-favourite sister (also, being my own godmother); I have my probably-favourite uncle to introduce me to further early lessons in madcap humour and to the world of science-fiction in its infancy, with the likes of John Wyndham, Isaac Asimov, Kurt Vonnegut et al; there also comes the first assumption of some mantle of responsibility, as I bring in the cattle myself, to set up and commence milking on those rare afternoons when the adults manage to oversleep their after-lunch naps; we enjoy the novelty and lasting ecstasy of giant field-mushrooms fresh from the paddock, pan-cooked with butter and a drop of vinegar, for breakfast. It is the early days of black and white television, and the reception here, nestled between Wingham and Taree and these surrounding hills, is always a touchy and unreliable business ... I remember the strand of aerial wire slung between two tall bamboo poles, leading to a dual-wire cable dangling inside the house. Tuning into the channel consists of randomly-sliding several separate sleeves of aluminium foil along the twinned aerial flex, until the best result for the nevertheless still-ghostly image accompanied by a hissing, crackling white-noise reception is obtained.

Rats are rife (in a large part, because of that mountain of corn ears sitting in the heart of the barn) and on some evenings, while watching the snowbound television broadcasts of the BBC's hilarious (if-one-could-but-see-and-clearly-hear-them), Christmas pantomimes, our rapt attention is often broken by the explosive bang of yet-another rat trap doing its job out on the verandahs, claiming a new victim. During these brief seasons, we escape into another world, where time slips by slowly as we merge into the rural existence, dip our hands into it – collecting fresh eggs from the remote henhouse; carrying the night-soil can, equiped with the post-hole auger, into yet another very green paddock in order to bury the week's contents; bearing the bright stainless-steel urn up to the house each morning, with cream brimming the top of the new, still-warm milk; collecting crickets from under dry cowpats, to use as bait for fishing the local creek; picnicking under the trees on fresh-cooked rabbits and amble geese from the fields and waters of the farm and refreshing ourselves in the coastal waters of the little inlet at Harrington, where my uncle's parents have retired. Looking back, these were perhaps primitive but still-innocent times and afforded simple pleasures – hard to discern and appreciate now, in this Brave New World of Everything – where everything is expected, if not demanded, now! ... the helter-skelter rushed age of 'I want it now' is fast upon us – and I must wonder just how far we have truly come.

* * * * *

ON THE EVE OF AND the turning-over into puberty, I was given my first taste of the road which lay before me. That dear uncle was kind to me and treated me as an equal, a friend, as he always would through the years lying ahead of us ... he expanded my taste for literature in several new directions aside from sci fi, cultivated an appreciation of the sort of loony humour or specialised satire embodied in that of the everlasting Goons and Stan Freberg, reinforced my fledgeling love for jazz (as had done also, my mother's younger brother, Dudley Graham) with the likes of Miles Davis and

Dave Brubeck and instilled in me, my earliest concept of taking personal responsibility for my actions, in a gentle fashion which until that time, had not been entirely obvious to me. These three or four seasons of summer holidays at the farm, slotted-in and combined happily with those seemingly-endless collection of sea-stays on Currumbin Hill, to create the most potent legacy of sight, smell and sound memories, around which my childhood revolved ... and slowly evolved, locking themselves forever into my core being.

The Esplanade, Currumbin Beach, circa 1950.

Elephant Rock & Currumbin Beach, circa 1950.

On the back steps at 'Furlough', Currumbin, circa 1950.

With Jan, behind 'Furlough', Currumbin, circa 1954.

MY FATHER'S GHOST: A MEMOIR

With Jan at Natural Arch, Springbrook, circa 1954.

With Jan, on Currumbin Beach, circa 1957.

4

The Avalanche of Adolescence

ON THROUGH THE GATE OF PUBERTY, blindly we ran, while our adolescent years rose up before us and trundled themselves in with no extraordinary show of drama ... the maelstrom of change might have surged about us but I am sure we rode about its edge on a largely-even keel - so far as I can recall, from the safe distance of this ever-advancing age. But then, at that singular point in development, there appear to be some large blank spots in this remnant, rusty memory bank - it's possible this might be blamed on the hormonal chaos which attends the average adolescence? Not that we consciously recognise it at the time ... just a random thought now, with the late benefits of hindsight.

In any case, adolescence had arrived ... and there I was, off to high school. Back in that long-ago, now almost-prehistoric past (much of history appears to be very-readily, very-quickly forgotten in this current age – an age of media-driven superlatives; when this day's current events become presented in terms which suggest that they never transpired to this degree in the past, or if they did, they were never as terrible as today's event ... and so, when the latest Brisbane flood rises up for instance, it is so, so tragic for so many and one might never imagine that there ever was such an all-enveloping flood in 1974, or in 1893 for that matter, when people just cleaned up and got on with their lives ... but, forgive me, I digress), high school was entered on completion of primary grade eight. By that time, I had already decided on my preferred career path and happily for me, the Brisbane State High School at South Brisbane, above all other state high schools, offered the optimum combination of subjects to provide for university entrance into architecture. It was by no accident perhaps, that quite a number of my fellow students at 'State High' were to join me there in the architecture faculty, upon graduation. My family lived out of the catchment for the school but out of consideration for my long-term goal, I was granted permission by the school, to attend. The memory of those adolescent years might be hazy but I carry nothing but good memories of those four secondary school years and I ever-continued to carry a quiet pride in 'Our State High' ... and bore especial gratitude for George Lockie, our much-loved and respected headmaster – as did continue many to revere him: generations of students both before and beyond our own.

Academically, I manage to be more than sound. Socially and physically, I am uncertain – as I imagine were many of us back then. Subsequently, I have no interest in and even avoid, all sporting activities, (upon final graduation, with better than average results,

George will remind me of this failing with a fatherly chide: 'You know Drew, you'd have certainly been a prefect if only you had just played a little sport.' As the only non-private school member of the GPS schools fraternity, State High prides itself on its history of combined excellence in both academic AND sporting fields ... and is very competitive in its strivings, as are all other GPS schools.) much-preferring my books and music. I guess I was and remain, reclusive and introvert, in spite of greatly-liking people and their company. Friday afternoons involve, for the majority, activity in either a sport or the school army cadets and air cadets. None of these really appeal to me at all. I seek to ease the burden by electing to join the army cadet band (where they march and play their instruments or when not doing that, they practice dashing through imaginary gunfire to dive and then hit the deck, as heroic medical bearers – this promises to be more desirable than marching, parading and going off to a shooting range to suffer the back-kick from elderly .303 rifles). My only problem here in the band is that, try as I might, I can extract no more than a pathetic 'blurp' from the cone of my bugle and resort in the main, to a poor display of mime.

Sooner or later, someone of significance is going to tumble to my charade. I am miserable in my faux bugler role and when the time comes to be sent off to the annual weekend army cadet camp with all its horror tales of boot-blacked privates of new recruits, I am terrified and escape, feigning illness at the last minute. I have to do something. Suddenly, through some now-forgotten but then-most-fortunate accident, I become aware of the existence of the school choir as an alternative to the sanctioned Friday after-noon activities. To sanctuary I and my vocal chords fly and with that, soon comes my introduction to Gilbert & Sullivan ... with 'Pirates', 'Pinafore' and 'The Mikado' all featuring. In all honesty, I never come to harbour any life-long passion for these works as any consequence of this ... but at the time, the choir suits my purposes conveniently and pleasurably – and pieces from those shows do remain lodged, even now, in my synapses somewhere. I have selected fourth year piano as an additional Junior subject and by now am quite au fait with the reading of music, as well as having gained an established, enduring love of classical composition – this manages to be happily-balanced alongside the new popular music of the era: The Beatles, Stones, Beach Boys et al. And with them, there comes also the still-emerging phenomenon of the folk era, Pete Seeger, Arlo Guthrie, Bob Dylan, Peter Paul and Mary, Donovan and all whom that genre carries to us in the darkened coffee houses, candles dripping and guttering in old wine bottles, cigarette smoke hanging lazily in the air, strumming guitars, often sadly-twanged ... oh, the idealistic romance of it! Bohemia and beatniks are de rigueur; the best of them sporting felt berets and thin, weedy goatees, corduroy trousers and turtle-neck sweaters.

Meanwhile, girls remain fearsomely-attractive but no less of a mystery to the gormless me: an attraction, which I have harboured from a very young age. While our newly-energised, hormone-driven libidos torment and confuse us, at school most of us are confronted daily by the godlike mythologies resting on the school's select-few of perfect physical specimens, boys and girls who, it is claimed, for the eyes and ears of us untouched lesser mortals, to have 'the reputation'. In retrospect, I suspect the reality may have been much-larger than life but to myself, clutching then, at a romantic disposition and with a host of hormonal changes raging away in the never-to-be-ignored background, it was a torment for one who lacked the confidence to seriously make any initial move on the object of affection or desire. I do have a number of 'girlfriends' and would-be-if-only girlfriends, during these tumultuous years, most of whom are garnered from my local church youth group. When I reconsider this, there are actually (the others remaining as idle wishful daydreams) only two, both of whom live almost adjacent to the church itself. There is Roberta, a gentle soul who will eventually die one day of cancer before she is very far into her twenties. She is followed by Suzette: tall, swingingly-bobbed blonde with large glasses and a willowy figure, along with whom my Jewish friend, Tony and I briefly seek to form a folk-singing trio. She has a gawky sense of personal style, wears large-brimmed hats with aplomb and will go on to become a pharmacist and marry a doctor. Both girls come from families with friendly and responsive parents, who treat me with kindness and affection. In this moment, so many years later, the memory of them and the houses they lived in, resurface briefly as if it were only yesterday – and one often wonders whatever became of all these people whom one knew and then lost to the detritus of the fleeting years.

Life at school does have its lighter side. Being in Brisbane's West End which contains a colourful mix of post-war migrant families, particularly those of Mediterranean origins, plus some of the early refugees from the newly-formed Soviet bloc, the student body here holds a rich mixture, often of rebels and pranksters blessed with humour, intelligence and sporting prowess. There exists a host of fellow students and teachers, a large number of whom will leave marks of certain indelibility to bridge the passage of the years. Small incidents continue to survive that passage of time like pages from our own Tom Brown's Schooldays or the William stories. Robert Comninus sits in our homeroom alongside his supposed friend, Peter Blums ... here, the diminutive Blums quietly slips Robert's lunch from his briefcase each day and devours it, having already eaten his own – until one day, Robert poetically seizes justice by substituting Sunlight soap slices for the cheese in his sandwiches and Blums finally gets his comeuppance, rushing out of the room to find the nearest drinking fountain. There are rats observed down in the garden bed just below our homeroom windows and one classmate attempts to fish for them, using a bent safety-pin with bread on the end of a long thread, drawn out from the fabric of his striped school tie. White mice are bred and fed in one of our homeroom lockers with scraps cadged from the tuckshop, until the stench in the room becomes unbearable.

The names of my compatriots alone, illustrate the endless variety of ethnic origins ... Dimitriou, Blums, Gollikov, Goulevitch, Tanton, the Mitchell twins, Howland, Saki, Ponomorenko, Morgan, Kildey, Cahill, Gerlic, Jurasnic, Conomos, Comninus, Hartley, Thompson, Topping, Diplock, Stanley, Moss. Sadly, many of the quirks and school traditions of those years would seem now to have been erased from history's pages, perhaps never to be remembered unless you were there. I suspect that our current increasingly-sanitised times will hold no further place for such foolishness. Revolution Day springs to mind – if my memory serves correctly, this was set for re-enactment, accompanied by its mostly-harmless prankster undertakings, on the first Friday following the Head of The River: the annual GPS rowing regatta – a high point in the school's sporting calendar. This was a time of unbridled mischief: a time when teachers were hung in effigy from the school flag pole; toilet bowls were cracked by a liberal detonation within by large fireworks; and the janitor locked out while he carried out maintenance on the parapeted roof of the main three-storied building (safe and secure, albeit), until he was finally rescued; our popular maths teacher, John (Nino – after Nino Culotta in the then-popular comic novella, 'They're a Weird Mob') Cullody's blue Volkswagen was manfully lifted and carried by a group of burly students to be wedged end to end, neatly between a pair of trees ... all truly-harmless fun then but in this squeaky-clean, uber-correct present, a memory best-erased. We seem now, to be entrenched in such an overwhelming seriousness where fun manifests in the sharing of noisy, herd-like tribal rituals and where our publicly-accepted humour is less than unfunny, relying inevitably on inane recitals of the most-ordinary complaints, punctuated inevitably by a barrage of expletives from which any humour appears to be derived. I fear that few can now support much time or place for our then-silliness, in these oh-so-serious times where childhood and youth seem to hold little or no productive place other than as something to be passed as quickly as possible, so as to move on to the most-profitable material station in life which one can occupy, all with the aid of enhancing technology from the ever-present 'internet of things' ... and where the spectre of litigation constantly looms over one and all, to curtail and gag so many aspects of our more-innocent and human activities. Suddenly, there is no age of innocence remaining, while we simultaneously bear the burden of an explosion of seriously-deadly recreational drug usage, along with disturbingly regular abuses of the Pandora's box of new phenomena contained in the so-called 'social' media – amongst other aberrations of our era ... 'Oh Brave New World that hath such people in it!'

But again, I digress – a lifelong trait of mine.

* * * * *

TEACHERS LIKEWISE, left fine imprints on memory – warmly, humorously, fondly. As with many episodes of my life, I find myself capable of remembering only the best – the positive and the good moments. I'm sure there must have been dark sides to many things but if these exist, they do not appear to have left any conscious scars in my overall awareness. Among these teachers there springs to mind Chas Walker, our English teacher: tall and clean-cut, glasses, likeable, droning his way through Joseph Conrad's 'Lord Jim' – putting half of us to sleep as he reads on and idly fingers an old, pencil-drilled hole in the top of one front desk (one of many, in the older desks in our year's homeroom) ... only to abruptly freeze mid-fingering, as he discovers the hole to be dammed from below with a wad of old chewing-gum and filled from above with a pool of fresh spittle. Non-plussed, he freezes only momentarily and then continues reading, whilst wiping his damp digit dry, slowly across the desktop ... nothing is said, no comment offered. And then there is Johnny,'The Major', (in the school cadets, that is) Hunt, our maths teacher: much older and wearing a perpetually-leaking blue biro, draining the stain of its innards across his white shirt's pocket every day, as he responds to a constant need of his to dash out and cross the road to post a letter ... while we are left alone, struggling to solve the algebraic equation he has placed on the board for us to occupy ourselves with. During this time, his progress to the postbox is monitored on high, from our overlooking home room window, while one of our top jokers swiftly alters the equation's answer, thus compromising his working of the sum upon returning. In this moment, he performs a surprised double-take, from the bottom, back to top of the board and down again ... and I often wondered whether he was in fact, on to us and fully aware of the ruse.

    And now, there comes to mind Perry Leach, our chemistry master, who spends any spare moments in class checking his racing guide, while his chemistry-lab class proceeds to 'unwittingly' concoct explosive gels in their test-tubes (or so he informs us with a mild warning, which only incites more experimentation) and quietly slip watered-down acid-filled burettes into each others trouser pockets. I become aware of this practice one day as my pocket is filled with what I take to be warm water, only to discover some days later (when the lining of the pocked has metamorphosed into a fragile, tissue paper-like fabric), that it contained diluted sulphuric acid. Und jetzt kommt unsere Herr Hermann Macdonnell: our German master who, for a time, fills me with a sound grounding in that language, which I do manage to excel at through these two years and in that time, he enthusiastically feeds my fledgling interest in psychology, by the loaning of some of his books on that subject, including hypnosis – such works as 'The Search for Bridie Murphy' and other similar studies of the time.

For a brief moment, there appears a Miss Sparkes: a stocky, athletic-looking teacher of yet-another field of mathematics. With her short-cropped, flaming red hair, she disappoints us all by not being in the least, intimidated by the host of fat grasshoppers one day released in class after our lunch break ... rather, she calmly marches about the room, snatching them from the air mid-flight and hurling them out through the open window. And who could ever forget our staid and proper art teacher, Alma Pleyton, as she skims at the very speed of light over each and every declared 'this-is-a-nude-picture' example in our set book, to hover ecstatically over more modest reproductions of still lives, interiors, landscapes, even abstracts, in our 'History of Art' set volume of ponderous bulk and weight. There, she will deliver her own notes at such a speed that we can barely write down everything in time ... our notebooks, we label at this point, with the title 'Pleyton Pace' (a reference to the risqué television weekly, 'Peyton Place': a television soap opera, popular during these times ... the contrast of 'risqué' here, with Alma herself, being an obvious one). Enter finally, our Harry Atwell, another English teacher, who must suffer from elevated blood pressure – for he has a fat purple worm of a vein which winds itself across his left temple and whose growth, his pupils cruelly seek to encourage for their own entertainment, by misbehaving to such an extent that he will redden with a flush which sends the vein into supernova ... how he survives this constant goading and lives, is one of nature's very own marvels.

* * * * *

SO PASS THESE YEARS of 'The High School, The Good Old High'. For the first two years here, I am the academic ruler of my own class, topping every term – for the latter two years, I manage to backslide into second place. There comes at one time in the close of my junior year, a nomination by my peers for the coming role of prefect; which eventually remains unfulfilled due to a robust sporting lassitude on my part. I evade the 'manly' activities by taking refuge in choral byways. I have school friends in the main, of similar retiring natures and in their company, I learn to smoke and we idle away some of our free time by rambling over Brisbane's Mount Cootha under the mild delusion that we are prospecting for gold; by diving for tossed coins on Saturday afternoons at the local Stones Corner pool; or just 'hanging-out' together at each others' homes. I remain entrenched in the weekly patterns at my family's Methodist church – sing in one, then two of our church choirs and occasionally stand in to conduct one of them; on occasions filling-in for the absent church organist. I attend religious instruction as a matter of course, at school on Thursdays and attend a Billy Graham rally one evening in the lovely (of a true architectural loveliness) St Andrew's Church in the city's Ann Street, with a bundle of my peers from our local church youth group.

Diminished by the enviable, though mythical-perhaps, holders of the 'reputation' amongst the gossip groups at school, I and a goodly number of my fellows, remain virgins. Man has just ventured into space and John Fitzgerald Kennedy is shockingly-dead. Martin Luther King Jnr will soon follow. When moments of teenage rage stir within me, I exorcise it by thrashing out a Beethoven sonata on our home piano ... it is remarkable how calming the playing of that music becomes after a couple of pages of Ludvig Van's score – then the playing becomes less fevered and more sensitive. 'Ludvig Van' should be marketed as one of the best of sedatives and all hormone-racked adolescents taught piano. By the end of these years, and in spite of some backsliding, I manage to secure the Commonwealth Scholarship which I have set my sights on – the reward which will ensure my entry into Queensland University and my future as an architect. This is the moment when 'our George Lockie' will deliver his historical prefect edict to me on my 'We sing the High School' - sporting shortcomings.

Somewhere in these sunset days of my high school years, when I am about sixteen, our sibling-count is increased to four by the arrival of Bronwyn Ellen, the baby of the family. Suddenly, with some semblance of now feeling to be an adult in the presence of this tiny bundle, I take a personal pride in being able to collect her from the cot when she awakes, change her nappies (with that, goes the less-than-savoury duty of hosing them off in the downstairs laundry and adding them to the tub, to soak) and when she graduates to a highchair, feed her. She is quiet, on the whole and uncomplaining when she wakes, as she sits in her cot, idly-twisting her hair around her finger and leaving a collection of neat, detached ringlets strewn over the mattress about her. Half a dozen years later, she will for a time, slide away into the role of that very-annoying kid sister, as I struggle with young adulthood.

For the moment, my pubescence is now a thing of the past and adolescence is fast-drawing to a close. As Trevor Howland had marked the end of my primary school years, so dear George Lockie signs off on my secondary years. Each of them left with me an enduring, positive and respectful fondness. It is only in this moment that I realise how we all really, have a strong need for father figures – in addition to the one we biologically own. This does in no way, lessen the role and influence of our mothers for us, but anthropologically, I suspect we males do often find ourselves acquiring a series of male role models to assist in guiding us at different stages through life. Aside from my own father, Trevor Howland, Herman Macdonnell and George Lockie assumed those mantles along the way ... along with some others who would, at some point or other, come to enter in upon that later life stage and leave their mark.

With Jan & Glenys, with a new sister, Bronwyn at Yeronga, 1963.

MY FATHER'S GHOST: A MEMOIR

JUNIOR 6
Back Row: J. Stanley, D. Melville, J. Spring, B. Drew
Third Row: P. Moss, S. Colville, W. Dickenson, P. Colclough, A. Glossop, A. Beswick, M. Self
Second Row: R. White, P. Blums, G. Bruback, R. Comninus, V. Orloff, J. Watson, A. Goulevitch, C. Meyers
Front Row: G. Gould, G. Kildey, T. Mossel, W. Hickey, R. Tanton, G. Welch, A. Osipovitch, P. Ponomarenko, C. Clark

My Junior year at Brisbane State High School, 1962.
My sister, Jan, has a crush on Peter Blums and Alec Goulevitch (who will be
mentioned again later), and she marks them accordingly.

SENIOR 4

Back Row: R. Colombo, T. Mossel, J. Dimitriou, C. Meyers, G. Wheeler, A. Talbot, A. Goulevitch, G. Bell.
Middle Row: A. Glossop, R. Nolan, B. Drew, R. Lacey, R. White, R. Carey, L. Hinsch, G. Kildey, P. Cahill, J. McGarry.
Front Row: G. Jordan, A. Osipovitch, R. Comninus, J. Matthews, R. Tanton, R. Blums, J. Taylor, P. Cox, T. Gerlic.

My Senior year at Brisbane State High School, 1964.
Seven of us will pursue architecture at the University of Queensland in 1965.
My picnicking & folksinging (with Suzette) friend, Tony, sits Front Right.

MY FATHER'S GHOST: A MEMOIR

SENIOR 8
Back Row: P. Hack, M. Lange, I. Sari, A. Ballantyne, R. Nicholls, L. Davidson, D. Howland, N. Ponomarenko, F. Smith.
Third Row: J. Hutchison, P. Dun, J. Gillies, M. Pavlos, A. Braunholz, B. Blair, A. Lipski, S. Spencer.
Second Row: G. Neilsen, C. Martin, R. Abell, M. Rudnev, N. Ochert, S. Cernak, N. Palun, M. O'Brien, P. Fischer.
Front Row: C. Burns, B. Rajewska, V. MacKenzie, A. Panos, R. Canning, J. Schubert, S. Wilson, P. Dare, L. Findlay, J. Gillies, D. Olive. *Absent:* C. Nugent, R. Wells.

The girls of my Senior year at Brisbane State High School, 1964. Inger Sari & Dianne Howland steal hearts from all and sundry, while Carol Burns, a future friend & theatre legend, sits front row, left.

With Suzette at her BGG Senior Formal, 1964.

PAGE 74

5

A Fortunate & Higher Education

AND SO OPENED THE TERTIARY YEARS: the parting of the doors to perception ... and to further confusions. I do believe I have been fortunate to have lived when I did. We were spared the first-hand trauma of war at our doorstep and the privations which attend such times. In the wake of the war, there did follow a period of austerity and the need for restraint in recovery but they were now accompanied by an assurance of safety, with a confidence in and optimism for, the future. There would of course, be other wars: in Korea, while I was still developing somewhere in my infancy and later, in Vietnam, when I was living through my tertiary years (both of these were other people's wars, the latter case being clearly-argued by the musical of those times, 'Hair') - and over much of that bridging period, and beyond, hung the spectre of The Cold War with its attendant uncertainties; these in some instances, extending to almost national paranoias. Luxuries in those early post-war years were thin on the ground and since even the simplest necessities had to be worked for and earned, they were never taken for granted – and thus, for most, they were respected and valued; nothing was ever expected as a right. Ours was a creative age – perhaps for the final time, one of complete autonomy for our human brains and the non-augmented products of their imaginings and reasonings ... and in that, and in the enjoyment of it, dwelt the elements of a final and closing age of innocence.

These university years at Brisbane's St. Lucia campus undoubtedly saw my own mind opened in a free and independent manner for the very first time. Still lacking any firm sense of confidence, identity and perhaps judgment, I felt my way with uncertainty, as was my nature ... self-promotion always remained a stranger and an unjustified, unwarranted concept for me; then, as now. And while I possessed the intelligence to be in that place of learning, socially and scholastically, I hid. But I managed in time to gently make my uncertain, halting way through it.

Being in such a protected and self-contained institution of autonomous intelligence and learning, cannot help but to rub off on its constituents. Suddenly, I discover a slowly-emerging awareness of who I am and of where I have come from – and I have questions. From the sphere of life at St. Lucia, I carry no memory of any obvious or concerted discussions regarding religion or politics ... they must exist somewhere but not in the everyday climate which surrounds me. The first three years of my architecture course are as a full-time day student and it is, in the main, a carefree and easygoing life. My Commonwealth Scholarship, aside from paying my fees for the privilege of being here, also provides me with a small living allowance (means-tested, as I recall) and I think I spend much of this allowance at the University Bookshop ... and not just on books concerning architecture. I indulge my newfound curiosity to the fullest: more books on psychology, anthropology, sociology, the Greek myths, contemporary literature and philosophy ... Masters and Johnson, Kinsey, Robert Graves, Orwell and Huxley, Robin Boyd, Donald Horne, Jean Paul Satre, Franz Kafka, Alberto Moravia, Joyce Carey and a host of playwrights, from Ibsen and Chekov to Euripides and back ... to David Williamson and other emerging playwrights. Our bookshop contains a smorgasbord for a young, questing mind. It is in this very-random opening-up of consciousness, that the mighty kraken of questioning awakes. How can I, raised as a Christian, have cause to be so absolute in my, let's face it, 'learnt beliefs'? Surely it is a matter of fate, rather than faith, which brought these credos into my world. Had I been born and raised a Buddhist, Hindu, Jew or Muslim, would I not believe just as fervently in one or the other of those faiths as being the only true one? Even within the Christian faith, there exist so many variations, each one proclaiming to be more legitimate than the other. So convinced am I at this time, of the vagaries of accidents of birth, that I write a letter straightway to the head of my own church, formally resigning as a confirmed Christian and leaving myself open to becoming some variation of, I suppose, agnostic. Likewise, I remember during these times of muted socialist hysteria, expressing the thought (which I probably continue to hold in some form as a certain basic truth) that, 'it is not Soviet communism which we should fear, but the subtle results of American-style capitalism, which will certainly become more overwhelming, all-consuming, with stealth and in a covert fashion, than this feared communism can ever hope to be, in that they draw upon the fundamental human weakness of avarice and covetousness to attain its ends ... ultimately, laying claim to our world – with even communism, through its upper echelons, succumbing to its wiles' (this was then 1967 and in time, even McDonald's made it to Moscow).

Thus, I came to think and reason beyond what I had been simply taught up until that point in my life. This was fostered in a fundamental environment of open enquiry, encapsulated by the best of traditional universities the world over – something which older universities have always been about ... something which I fear, is perhaps being lost in this present age where tertiary institutions suddenly seem to proliferate and become, more than anything, yet another business (even to the point where a degree or even a doctorate, might to all intents and purposes, effectively be purchased from some obscure institutions and their validity never questioned by others ... until the wheels fall off). On many public levels, our lives have truly entered the age of 'spin'.

* * * * *

MY COURSE is to occupy six years of my life (seven, as it eventually transpires) – the first three of these will be as a full-time day student; for the final three, I am to be an evening student, working by day for an architect's office (this is a mandatory prerequisite for continuing with the course into the following years), in order to acquire a level of practical experience. These initial years make for a relaxed and enriched time. Our first day in this world of higher learning opens with an address by our very-first year master, William Carr, something of a young, rebellious, southern intellectual ... he introduces himself thus: 'My name is Bill Carr. You may call me Mr Carr, you may call me Bill, you can call me Son of a Bitch – I don't care.' He then proceeds to advise us that architects should 'design, if not make, their own clothing' – which, a number of us, later proceed to do. He concludes this first lesson by playing for us, a very-early tape recording of Barry Humphries, describing 'A Nice Night's Entertainment' with darling Norm, as related to her bosom friend and bridesmaid, Madge Allsop, by the soon-to-be more-than-great, Edna Everage of Melbourne's Moonee Ponds. We attend our lectures and resolve our design assignments in our studio space during the days, as well as into some evenings, accompanied by half-bottles of claret or Galway Pipe Port which we keep along with handmade artistic stoneware beakers in the drawers of our homeroom desks.

On Friday afternoons for two years, we have a subject called free-drawing ... we are divided into two groups which alternate their weeks by drawing life models, male and female, in the studio when they are not out in the gardens or the city, sketching plant-life or buildings and passers-by. The life drawing is popular and we extend our Friday afternoons into some evenings, at our lecturer's home or the city studio of the Contemporary Art Society where we arm ourselves with charcoal and newsprint, claret and model, while the model's husband sits quietly in one corner strumming out Flamenco guitar for us ... Bohemia lives. The CAS is having a party, a Greek party and we are all invited ... if we provide the decor. For weeks leading up to the event, students sit in the sun outside our homeroom with hammers and cold-chisels, carving metopes into paving slabs purloined from the stock laid up for the new footpath, Greek swords are formed and forged in brass, helmets and shields beaten from mothers' copper washtubs and a convincing chariot welded up, bearing a kangaroo motif painted on its side ... a trailer licence will be obtained enabling it to be towed by its creator's American convertible, from the St Lucia campus across town to the Art Society's venue at Kangaroo Point – as it rumbles along noisily on its bare steel wheels down Coronation Drive, it will be pulled over by the police; not for the absence of a licence but for the toga-clad, helmeted character standing with a large battle axe in the chariot (the trailer licence did not cover for a passenger). Our arty hosts prove more decadent than our green selves and the retsina and ouzo flow with such abundance that a number of very sore heads greet the new day back on campus.

There is an abundance of spare time available to us, which is mostly-absorbed by innumerable cheap coffees and cigarettes at The Refectory when nothing else is happening and by visits to 'The Bookshop' (and lo, there worked behind the enquiries counter in those times, a petite and tidy young woman, comely and passing fair in both looks and nature, bearing the almost-musical name of Liberata Pizzica – known to most as Libby. It needs no saying that I am just a tad smitten by her; and she does prove to be more than pleasant to chat with at every opportunity). I am elected to represent my year at QASA meetings (this being the Queensland Architectural Students' Association, on whose enduring logo of those years is a beautifully-stylised Egyptian scarab) ... and in a very short while there also comes an involvement with Dramsoc, the university's drama society.

These are to prove to be among the richest of times with Dramsoc, introducing an equally-rich parade of characters, some of whom will eventually go on to greater things in the theatrical world. The high point of my involvement centres around a mixed review named 'Pucker Up – Here Comes A Big Red Kiss', in which I stumble gauchely through a couple of minor roles. The show's driving force, principal-writer and director is a very-talented and likeable young man named Rodney Fisher (now Rodney Fisher AM) who will go on to claim a highly-esteemed future as a multi-disciplined theatre director with, amongst other directorial credits, shows featuring the wonderful Robyn Archer ... and a range of achievements in all facets of theatre too numerous to expound. The review's production and subsequent run at the old Avalon Theatre close by the university is exciting and enormous fun as we work hard at putting together all of Rodney's very original material, which continues forming and further-developing itself daily, as we launch ourselves into the project, living for the moment an existence separate from our studies. Wonderful costume shirt-tops are made from colourful geometric-patterned cotton fabrics sourced from Jules & Jim in Sydney; we get to keep these and mine remains a favourite piece of memorabilia for many years afterwards. We even have an original theme song which is sung in the show and recorded for radio publicity by our own Christina Koutapedis, who vamps up the number beautifully (her mother is Helena Kay, of the city's famous dress salon, which she herself will later in life, take charge of; in the interim, she will star in 'The Owl and The Pussycat' at Gowrie Hall's Twelfth Night Theatre). We reward our hard work with moments of play in our occasional cast parties. Ike and Tina Turner are new on the scene and their current album 'River Deep, Mountain High' resounds across the neighbourhood as we bop and stomp our way endlessly through midnight and beyond. These are, in retrospect, such innocent but the very best of times.

There exists a host of other very talented theatre people in and around our Dramsoc in these days, including the lean and lithe Doug Anders, a graduate of NIDA, whose own particular special area-of-interest lies in that of stage movement ... and he can be unmistakably-glimpsed moving through the streets of our still-fledgeling city with all the fluidity of a panther on the prowl. He displays his considerable acting talents (and mischievous sense of humour) in a number of prominent roles in 'Pucker Up' and is an easy-going man, easy to befriend. In days when I possessed more body-flexibility than I now own, I take part in the weekly movement classes he conducts for a small group and take great pleasure in accepting the role of set and graphics designer for him, as we stage Euripides' drama, 'Electra', in the original Twelfth Night Theatre on Wickham Terrace in the days of their early artistic director, Joan Whalley ... and completely dismantle their existing proscenium theatre arch and stage in its entirety in the process, so that we might stage the play in three-quarters round. The theatre never does manage to be restored to its original state and continues to be used, somewhat in a state of compromised limbo, before it is eventually relocated to a brand new theatre building in Bowen Hills, where it remains. This was a long time ago and I forget many of the names but I do remember that Electra's brother, Orestes, was played by a very talented young man named Ross Foley – very promising in the movement classes and one who would go on, I am told, to become a dancer with a Sydney dance company; Clytemnestra was played by Patsy McCarthy and Electra, by Diane Neale, while a young John Dommett played the messenger (something like thirty years will pass before I encounter John again, when his mother and mine occupy adjacent hospital wards) ... I do remember the role of Aegisthus as being distinctly unmemorable except for the young actor's bulk, since his only requirement was to play that of the king's corpse. My humble self had a walk-on appearance as one of the stretcher bearers for the king's weighty body.

At this time, I re-encounter a young woman named Carol Burns who had been a fellow student at Brisbane State High during my years there. We had been in the same year at the school but, with the strong segregation of the sexes demanded there in those days, her existence had escaped my notice at the time. She has by this time, been a promising acting protege of Twelfth Night's Joan Whalley. We do form a friendship which will resurface randomly with chance encounters over the years. She will in fact, go on to lead a distinguished career as an actress and a director, in television, film and stage. She is to become one of those grand ladies of Australian theatre, a station sadly cut short by her early death at the age of sixty-eight. I have always felt, that with the passing of the lovely Ruth Cracknel, that Carol had remained to fill her empty shoes in a credible way in the corridors of Australian theatre.

Whilst we are busily dismantling for all of time (until its eventual resumption to make way for the Turbot Street Expressway) the interior of Twelfth Night's Gowrie Hall, Joan Whalley and her theatre continue to form a fertile hub for the fostering of local talent. A young Shane Porteous and Michael Caton are performing across the road at Mark Twain's Theatre Restaurant in Ann Street and are regularly encountered at Gowrie, each laying the foundation for enduring careers in Australian theatre and film. Barry Otto is soundly setting off on his road to theatrical and cinematic stardom – and on the fringes of Dramsoc and Twelfth Night, just scraping in as the senior of these figures, is a young man by the name of Jack Thompson. Even in these times, he comes with something of an expansive background to his thespian pedigree – as a child, he has understudied for the film role of 'Smiley'; he has served a stint with the army; he has worked at Hayes Gordon's Ensemble Theatre in its early days in Sydney; he is reputed to be living in a menage a trois with two sisters and he is already bathed with a strong charismatic glow. Seven years my senior, he holds the gauche green me in awe: apt fodder for hero-worship ... I follow his progress about the campus, I smoke what he smokes (a compacted Dutch shag tobacco by the name of Neptune Brand in a pocket-sized, crushable matt, pale-blue, paper packet – this, rolled with Rizla liquorice papers) and attend on Sunday evenings, more-specialised stage-movement classes which he conducts at Gowrie Hall.

Here, impressively, he plays to us a tape containing a drum-by-drum build-up of varied, overlaid percussion tempos ... and he illustrates these by progressively isolating various parts of his body set to each tempo – fluttering hands, lunging shoulders, jerking neck, marching feet, wobbling knees, thrusting hips and arching spine ... every limb, extremity or joint maintains its impetus as yet another body part picks up on each new percussive beat as it makes its entry into a collective cacophony of sound which somehow, all manages to slot pleasingly together ... creating a visual and physical feat from which to draw wonder.

Needless to say, for a number of its early years, my application to my architecture course was richly balanced by this casual involvement on the thespian front. It was not a singular distraction. Many of our other architectural students also became involved in matters theatrical when once each year the Architects' Review was staged. Architecture, at least once-upon-a-time, was one of those career pursuits which were to open up a whole wide world of creative possibilities ... think of Aunty Jack, aka Grahame Bond. Many would step sideways at some point to shape-change to another career ... a small step to marine architect, landscape architect, industrial designer ... a larger slide to stage design, acting, dance, rock musician ... the world became a big, wide space and many moved into its broader domain. The architects' reviews were the brain children, in the main, of the fertile mind of the Sino-Australian architecture student, Willie Young (later to become William Yang), responsible for the overall direction and the bulk of the script-writing, ably-assisted by the musical input of one Ralph Tyrrell ... both of these personalities eventually moved beyond the reach of architecture into music, film and photography. These annual reviews were a mix of crazy, insane, irreverent skits and satirical sketches, along with full-on rock performances, with multi-level, moving, cantilevered platforms containing an array of musicians and singers, aka architecture students. They emerged under revue titles like 'Blue Owo' (derived from the adverts for a washing powder of those years, Blue Omo),

'High On A Hot Banana' (derived from Donovan's contemporary song Mellow Yellow) and 'Young Robert Zimmerman' (aka Bob Dylan). One must remember that these were, in the main, full-time day students with an abundance of spare time to lavish on creative side-stepping. One of these children, a wild young Ross Gilbert, would cut his incredibly-curly mass of unruly hair only once each year ... after the the revue was over for that year, in which instance he would always play the role of 'The Dog'. When the show was over, it entailed just one very-bold razor-close cut until same time next year.

* * * * *

DURING THESE EARLY YEARS of my course, I manage to supplement my modest government living allowance by working whenever term breaks from the university year give the opportunity. These are not fantastic or career-related jobs but they do provide a significant boost to my lean cash resources and broaden my freshly-emerging experience of life with a very different cast of characters. Every August, when the westerly winds blow away the last shards of winter, Brisbane conducts its annual Royal National Agricultural Show, affectionately known as 'The Ekka', an event which few locals or visitors ever miss. The long-established RNA Association organises and staffs most of the public and supporting facilities which accompany this spreading exhibition of crops and stock with its host of auxiliary, commercial hangers-on. Needless to say, much of this support staffing is a short-term affair and university students take advantage of its generous hourly rates – at least, those fortunate enough to secure a position at the outset ... once there, they can be assured of filling a continuing notch at this time, secured through the following years.

MY FATHER'S GHOST: A MEMOIR

My first season in this role sees me acting as a turnstile attendant at one of the many pay-gates giving entry into the grounds. I spend my eight hours collecting the then-still-moderate entry coinage from my little undercover cage, as the public proceed to tick over the rolling counters connected to the turnstiles, recording the visitor numbers for the day – on occasion, some more-amorous courting couples refuse to be separated by this act of entry and insist on squeezing through one gate together ... this, so transparently, provides them with an excuse for a moment of more intimate than usual contact, as they cram themselves sardine-like through the revolving gates to a day of boisterousness, dust, fun and flu. This role is surpassed the following year by a stint as a toilet attendant ... mounting my watch at the men's toilets adjacent the large cattle pavilion on the hill, I am required to keep my patch clean and sweet-smelling, while I collect a penny from those wishing to use a closed cubicle. I sweep and mop, replace toilet rolls and hand towels but I cannot bring myself to hang around inside, requesting pennies from burly strangers. I am miraculously spared any major spills during my stay and make sure my facility is kept properly stocked and sweet-smelling with liberal sprays of disinfecting perfume all around ... then I retreat to a sunny, innocuous place at a distance against the wall outside, while I pretend to have no connection with this duty and pray that no-one who knows me happens by.

My third year in this capacity, sees me engaged here as a night watchman. My duties are simple – I am given a vehicle delivery gate to guard each night, from 10pm to 6am ... that's all there is to it. I don't have to prowl around with torch and whistle in hand ... all that is required of me is to just be there ... in case a delivery truck should arrive during the night, requiring entry; whereupon I check his papers, unlock the gate and allow him in. This hardly ever happens during my vigil. It is freezing cold out there, dark and empty. I go to my allocated station each night, armed with a thermos of hot coffee, a large bar of chocolate, a book and a blanket - and with the hope that my particular gate allocation this night will give me a light to read by and a sheltered place out of the ever-present bone-chilling wind, preferably with some form of bench to sit on. The best thing about this posting is that working through these early hours, gives me access to a pay rate of time-and-a-half and for the nights either side of Sunday, this increases to double time. There is nothing difficult about the mission, just a degree of tedium and some mild discomfort; any thought of it being dangerous, isolated through the night like this, never occurs. This, being my final Ekka with the RNA before I move on out of day student status, provides more of a temporary topping-up of the coffers than ever happened before.

* * * * *

DURING THESE HALCYON day-student years, the long Christmas break from studies provides further opportunity to restock the larder. Here again, I am fortunate. Amongst my fellow choristers at our local church (while I still remain part of it during this initial year of self-discovery), there is an executive with Provincial Traders, then manufacturers primarily of margarine and Dixie frozen chickens - one Lloyd Weldon. Even though I will someday leave their church, they are all good, supportive people and Lloyd, knowing my position, offers me employment over the Christmas vacation at his factory. It is a lowly position in what is called The Yard Gang ... a miscellaneous bunch of mostly-rough, older diamonds who perform a myriad of lesser but necessary duties about the works. Every morning, we clock-on with our punch cards at the entry to our holding pen. Each worker's name is read out at the allocated hour by the supervisor, along with his area of duty for the day. I do have variety at least ... I find myself riding shotgun on the old blitz-wagon which lives again as the dedicated rubbish truck doing the rounds of the factory; or loading refrigerated lorries with large cartons of frozen chickens or margarine to then accompany them to the goods yards across in the city, where we unload them into refrigerated railway wagons; on other days, travelling down to the docks, where we are provided with wharfies' hooks to assist us in carrying across our shoulders, the enormous hard and lumpy hessian bags of copra from their pallet stacks, which we manhandle onto the backs of waiting flatbed trucks and accompany them back to the factory to then be unloaded again ... when it is not copra, it is hundredweight sacks of green peanuts ... or, horror, on one occasion, tightly packed, cloth bags of fishmeal (this is a fine greenish dust and it stinks - it is used as a component in producing the highly-nutritious pellets they manufacture to feed to the chickens - and the irritation I suffer from its dust, which will seem forever to be embedded in the clothes I wore that day, is responsible that evening, for the only bleeding nose I will ever experience).

For further variety as a member of this yard gang, I must stand through a long day before an endless overhead conveyor rail as once-chickens, stripped of their dignity, blood, feathers and innards, pass by me and I take my turn to relieve them of their heads: their last real vestige of chicken-hood. This is a depressing place, peopled with the only truly-rough element in the whole factory - here, the women are worse than the men and in this well-lit dark place, fights often break out amongst these harridans who will think nothing of taking a filleting knife (of which there are an abundance) to each other in their flashes of anger. The stainless steel troughs and floor of this vast abattoir are wet and continuously drained by a system of gutters and channels, all of which empty below into yet another port of call: an underworld which I must occasionally man. Here, in this netherworld, rolling on their sides, are two enormous double-screen-layered, stainless steel rotating drums with powerful water jets passing through them from all angles. Down this cylindrical corridor, proceeds all which finally remains of the charnel doings upstairs ... feathers, intestines, feet, heads – all carried down in the torrent to make their sorry exit from the world – on their way to the next. Our job in this crypt is to collect all of these now-very-clean remainders in 44gallon steel drums heavily-punched through from top to bottom, giant strainers for the water also exiting. We carry large, wide bristled brooms with which we seek to control the river of ex-life. When each large drum is brimming over, we must quickly roll it to the side, using its lower rim and swiftly replace it with an empty one before the floor can flood with rubbish. It is heavy work and messy, but everything is squeaky-clean by this stage – and it does have its moments of excitement when the rotating tunnel will suddenly empty but for a mere trickle of water. Then, we know our fate ... a lone, whole once-chicken has escaped from its death mooring on the conveyor and plunged into the Styx to take its stand, blocking the entire drainage works. We know what is to come next ... a giant outburst of water will be sent down to flush the culprit out and there, we bravely stand, brooms in hand, waiting to vainly hold back the tsunami of everything, which will rush upon us at any moment – and all we two gatekeepers are able to do is push back at the flood while it rapidly fills and overflows each drum and thence rush ankle-deep over the floor. It is exciting in its morbid way but cannot be called fun, as we broom and mop to clear away and collect the out-of-control overflow. Our amassed barrels of these mementos of chicken death will be collected from our cavern in their turn, to be cooked up and combined with the fishmeal we collect from the wharves to make 'tasty' pellets which will then be fed back to new generations of chickens. My rite of passage through this abattoir deprives me of any desire for commercially-produced chicken for a very long time.

Ever so occasionally, I am given cause to wonder why of all the people present in our lives at any particular time, this or that (often unprepossessing) person manages to leave an indelible imprint. I mean, some instances one can understand but a big ageing hulk of a fellow who drives a filthy old rubbish truck every day around a chicken and margarine factory? Big Jim does just that (the wonder is that I even remember his name), day in, day out. And it is he, for whom I ride shotgun on those days when it is my bolden duty so to do. He is no longer young: a big lump of a kindly diamond in the rough; probably muscular once, his shoulders are broad and his arms are meaty ... all covered under his navy singlet with fine, grey, curly down and he has a Ronald Coleman moustache. His dump-truck is a left-over from the war years: an old army blitz-wagon with a flattop back, on which we carry our rubbish bins. The vehicle has long-ago been relieved of its two doors, to better facilitate the constant jumping in and out at our ports of call ... these are where we collect the contents of rubbish bins from the upper and lower echelon lunch rooms, the offices, the laboratories and the chicken hatchery with its bins of hatched-out eggshells and the fluffy little yellow bodies of those who never quite made it to the nurseries. He drives this tank as if he is still back in a war zone and I cling to my seat for dear life. Having no doors, the interior is perpetually dust covered and he smokes moist Cavendish tobacco roll-your-owns which sit part-consumed and cemented in multiples, butt-down ash-up, by their own spittle on the dusty dashboard as he dashes off into each new collection point. We collect our haul and, once back in the wagon, he snatches up any one of his unfinished collection, thrusts it into his lips, relights it, puffs and stokes it back into life until the next stop is made.

There is always respite for an hour at lunch time when all of these mainly gentle, yard-gang roughnecks gather in their shady lunchroom cum locker-room, where most of them fill their free time playing cards. They seem to have established groupings and in any case, I do not join in ... I sit apart at my bench, unmolested and unnoticed, and read Robert Graves 'Greek Myths' complete with all of the notes and other annotations: a solitary observer of this, my own modern day pantheon of minor deities. I manage to make my way through both copies of these books while I serve out my tenure here.

* * * * *

THE FOLLOWING YEAR's Christmas break and the one following that, become more genteel in the manner of my employment and its surroundings. My Dad remains the power station's reliable Mister Fixit and they are in need of a draughts-person to catch up on all of their outstanding draughting requirements ... and I fit the bill perfectly. My skills are well-honed in that discipline by now and they have excellent facilities for one who is still working at home with a basic tee-square and board propped up on the kitchen table. Here, I work for the first time on very professional blue, waxed tracing linen, with a giant board having an adjustable stand and a proper drafting machine (and an electric eraser), tucked away in a quiet corner of their library – I am spoilt beyond belief. There are miles of electric circuitry designs waiting to be committed to the cloth ... along with a percentage of mechanical drawings of taps, valves and other devices for the workshops. Across the corridor from where I sit near the librarian, is the office of the station's chief engineer, Syd Durrington, a bright young electrical engineer who will eventually end his days in charge of the new Swanbank Power Station when it is later commissioned. He is relaxed and friendly and we form a happy working relationship, since I take most of my instructions from him. We chat away morning tea breaks while he talks enthusiastically of his latest culinary efforts for his fiancé. During my lunch breaks that year, I spend them chortling my way (mostly that is, until the true message in the latter part of the book, subtly makes its way to the surface) through Joseph Heller's 'Catch 22'. From this time on, I fulfil their drafting needs every semester break until my fourth year, when I enter full-time architectural employment. Such is my input here at Tennyson, that when the power station finally closes its doors and its smoke stacks, the drawers of the library's plan collection are full of my blue linen drawings and little else.

MY FATHER'S GHOST: A MEMOIR

Our set for 'Elektra' at Gowrie Hall's Twelfth Night Theatre, June 1967.

With Judith McCooey, a stage crew member for 'Elektra', 1967.
At the Architecture Students' Formal, Brisbane's Belle View Hotel that year;
Before it's later, swift midnight demolition by the Dean Brothers!

MY FATHER'S GHOST: A MEMOIR

With Sue Benson, librarian to the Architecture Department.
Dinner at the Mark Twain Theatre Restaurant, Brisbane, 1966.

With Christine at the Haynes' House Party for their new home;
Ascending the heights of Hamilton, Brisbane, 1967.

6

A Major Leap into the Unknown

SOMEWHERE IN THE LATTER PART of my third year, I manage to take unwittingly (as many were), a further life-changing step. A year or two ahead of me in our faculty there is one Graeme Johnston whose true love is theatre (and I believe he never completes architecture, opting eventually for a life in theatre as director, script writer, designer and costume designer: quite an all-round talent on the thespian front). Each year, he produces (on his own in all of the just-mentioned capacities) a Gilbert and Sullivan operetta to benefit the 'Xavier Home for Crippled Children' – and this particular year, it is to be their lesser-performed 'Patience'. The first I know of any of this is when he approaches me to play the role of the aesthetic poet,

Archibald Grosvenor who, along with a more-earthy poet, Reginald Bunthorne, vies for the love of a milkmaid, Patience. Grosvenor was a satirical rendering of the period's Oscar Wilde along with the accompanying mannerisms of the era ... Graeme presents me accordingly: in sky-blue velvet jacket with an exaggerated white lace collar, bleached bobbed hair, blue tights and pumps on my feet – such is the image presented, that my initial entry into each performance is greeted by a barrage of hoots and catcalls from the audience. This is all a novel experience for the tentative would-be-if-he-could-be young stage-struck student, occupying a primary role and a singing one at that. It is incredibly scary at the same time as being exciting and lots of fun. I have a fast change in the wings having been convinced by the professionally- and socially-jealous Bunthorne to become a very-commonplace young man, reappearing on stage decked out in the loudest and largest black and white check suit, boots and sporting a black bowler hat. Needless to say, the move backfires on the hapless Bunthorne when aesthetic poetry wins through and the bevy of young women, including Patience, continue to pursue the ever-charming Archibald Grosvenor, even in his common guise. And so, the mannerisms of the age triumph.

Tucked away somewhere in the ladies' chorus is a young woman, Catriona who, during the show's production period, very swiftly manages to claim me in real life, for her future self and before my fourth university year is to run its course, we are married. I am just twenty-one and probably as raw and green and feckless as a young man in these times can be. Much of what transpired to carry me into and through that wedded state was in retrospect, brought about by a very-naive simple hormonal response accompanying my own loss of innocence and its attendant pleasures, at the hands of one not in fact, so innocent ... rather than by any intellectual or common good sense. A little over four years later, I am to be single again, married in name only for the next few years until our decree nisi is finally enacted ... with the remnants of that brief union, a small blip on the screen of our lost histories.

* * * * *

BACK ON CAMPUS in the meantime, days in the Garden of Eden are about to draw to an end with the coming of fourth year: the switch from day student to evening student and the attendant taking-on of work within an architect's office, had arrived. So stringent was this requirement for our course, that if one was not thus employed by fourth year's end, continuation with the course could be suspended until the situation was remedied. There were offices ... and then there were offices. There existed at the time, one office – an architect of some charisma with modest but sound talent, working to an effective personal design formula – whose own ego was nevertheless matched perhaps by his keen opportunism – in that he engaged student employees who would actually be prepared to pay him for the privilege of working under him (as if he were some latter-day Frank Lloyd Wright – a considerably-stretched comparison). This was a rare instance but it was known to happen. One took what employment one could find then ... and was grateful.

My first job is in a small and insignificant office: that of a supposed architect who quickly, stutteringly, follows up his name with, '... I'm an architect, ... actually', upon every telephone introduction – and who, as was then termed, slipped in the back door; having no formal degree or diploma, a draughtsman in reality, who managed to pass the then Registration Board's formal examination and thus gain entry into the hallowed halls of architecture. He manages to survive on small, developer-driven, suburban shopping centres. I and the only other employee, Ian, swelter over our tee-squares and drawing boards through the summer months in the tiny airless space under the front of our employer's home – working away in a sharp, head-clearing atmosphere of ammonia fumes issuing from the early plan-printing machine which shares our workspace. We fill any idle intervals by perfecting our skills at shooting-down the many flies which invade our space ... our preferred weaponry being a rubber band stretched along one side of our scale rules – the deadly projectile, then to be released catching its targets in mid-flight. The almost-an-architect's young twin boys fill their own idle moments by hosing us through the high-set open windows: the only ventilation to our space; thereby often ruining hours of detailed work at the drawing board – this, their father dismisses with great jollity, declaring 'Well, boys will be boys. It's all good practice for you,' as we are forced to redo the plans. Needless to say, our rates of pay are lowly. Ian is eventually conscripted into the war of this time, only to spend his days dying of boredom in his local military office as a minor officer ... spared the dangers of actual conflict but consigned to spending his days with little to do but fill them by sharpening his pencils and reading the daily newspapers over endless cups of cheap coffee – one can only endure so much of that. It spoils the idea of architecture for him for all time and I believe he drifted elsewhere when finally released from his conscription.

I, in my time, will have my own marble drawn for the Vietnam conflict. I am kindly, spared. Since I am the holder of a Commonwealth Scholarship and am halfway through my course, my call-up is to be deferred until I graduate. By then, the war will be consigned to the dust of history ... except that is, for some who will continue to remember it down through the avenues of time, for the remainder of their lives. Fifty years later, the Black Dog of those years' aftermath continues to pursue a large number of them, quietly-unnoticed.

An old school chum and later, fellow architecture student at UQ, Alec, has his marble drawn at the same time as myself but he does not wait around to argue the issue. He runs – takes off, moves to Sydney, changes his name, enrols at that university to do a commerce course and marries. Alec comes from a good, white Russian family but has been something of a wild boy at school, often joyriding in stolen cars on weekends but somehow (even after making off with the car of an old lady who gently declined to press charges, in one instance), getting off lightly for his youthful exuberance and returning to school in a day or so. A number of my high school classmates had appeared in our lineup for architecture at the university and Alec arrived with them. For all his wildness, he is at his core, a decent being and a stalwart friend to all those fortunate enough to fall with him into that classification. His case summed up Vietnam for me, with the long shadow that it was to cast ... having escaped that fate for a brief and frail moment, he is eventually to be discovered, snatched up, rushed through basic training at Kapooka and sent off to the war ... only to be returned some weeks later, relieved of the best part of one forearm. This story for years, continued to speak reams to me of the pointlessness of that 'dirty little war', as the musical, 'Hair', so aptly proclaimed the intruded-upon conflict.

Some years later, I am to learn more of Alec's history through a mutual friend, a solicitor (now himself, prematurely dead of cancer) who will have a number of occasions on which to represent Alec. He had come back maimed by the war, completed his architecture course and quietly retired from the world to Stanthorpe, inland and close to the New South Wales border. It seems he had in fact been returned, a reluctant hero. Early in his tour of duty, his platoon is ambushed while on patrol and is badly shot up, leaving him as the only member of the group remaining in any condition to do anything at all; as he does with his one still-functioning arm. He manages to singlehandedly man a machine gun and hold the Viet Cong at bay until the helicopter gun ships arrive to rescue them. As the result of his perhaps desperate or gallant actions, not one of his group will lose his life on that day and Alec is to be aptly-decorated upon his return. Understandably, he suffers with shell shock from that point onwards, which does nothing to enhance his future life ... now, we have an in-tune-with-the-times all-embracing label (as we have for so many conditions in this brave new world) and we call it PTSD – an abbreviated label, as is so popular in our time-strapped times. It in essence, means much the same thing as it always did but the rabidly-political-correctness of our age often demands that we avoid the directness of telling the truth as it simply is and thus, seek to include every conceivable aspect of it and lodge the truth of the matter within elaborate short-cut labels ... the avoidance of calling a spade a spade, often draws more attention to the fact that it is a spade, than it would otherwise. I sometimes feel that this is gradually eroding much of our linguistic heritage, as some words take on totally new meanings while their original, age-old usages are now suddenly, in effect tabooed, sent into denial, deemed inappropriate. I find a great cultural loss and sadness in this sanitising and distortion of our English language – now also, being eroded BTW, by LOL (except that it's not funny), the emergent language of the OMG slick-thumbed screen-pass and emoticons – the tomb hieroglyphics of our age. But I diverge again ... as is and has been, my White Rabbit way.

* * * * *

AS THE FINAL DAYS of my fourth year of studies approach, I hover on the eve of my relatively short-lived wedded bliss. My end-of-year exams this year have been cut short by a heavy bout of German measles which only reveals itself while I am one hour into the seven-hour design exam which we must now face at this stage of the course ... 'So that's that then', I think to myself. I am to miss out also on the balance of my theory subject tests before I am recovered; and so, I resign myself to the fact that I will have to repeat this year's design subject, as well as most of the theory components. I suspect that my scholarship will not cover me for this repeat and that I will have to find the means somehow to fund it myself through the coming year.

What is not expected, will be the telephone call which comes to me at the office where I am now working, from my attentive year master, Hamish Murison - in which he requests me to sit for the design exam again. I had abandoned all hope as most of my assignments had been submitted late through the year and I was sure to fail. Hamish informs me that all I need to do in sitting for this post-exam, is to scrape a basic pass and I will be through the year and able to continue with my course. The only catch is, that I am to sit the exam on Friday: the day of my five o'clock wedding. Of course I accept it and secure a pass as it turns out, thus keeping my scholarship intact ... making this day a memorable day in more ways than one. After an earlier than usual start for normal exams, the demands of such an extended examination time are met in one sitting, without the usual break for lunch. My best man, Milan, is waiting to collect me afterwards in order to whisk me home to freshen and dress ... while a storm-burst half an hour before the wedding is sufficient to cleanly wash the pavement and see it dry again, just before the bride's arrival with her flowing train. With the adrenalin surge from the events of the day up until this moment, all that transpires from this point forward is experienced in a kind of numbed blur. The most regrettable part of which is that I manage to hear not one bar of the lovely collection of choral music, which my new father-in-law has arranged for his Conservatorium choir to sing - and with it, overlay our ceremony.

Basil has lavished such loving care upon its selection and arrangement and in the hours afterward, I come to realise with enormous disappointment, that not a note has registered in my benumbed brain.

So we are married, (for what that eventually proves to be worth) ... and a relatively-modest reception follows, which we tread our way through in a proper, low-key manner as I recall it now ... in all fairness, not a 'Dimboola', but a rather sober, restrained affair. I remain probably shellshocked from the crammed intensity of the day and in a benumbed mood, I await the moment when we can depart from this gathering of hail-fellow-well-met relatives and friends, for the sanctuary of our honeymoon flat in the middle of what is the cosy coastal town of Surfers' Paradise – not the overwhelming megapolis which it has become. I am twenty-one; we have no car of our own and I am yet to gain a licence even, to drive one. Our best man, Milan and his wife, Sue drive us there and stay with us this first night. So much else of these times blurs slightly now, when viewed fifty-odd years later. It seems to me that there remains little, if any, of the negative experiences of a life which I manage to carry around with me and overall, it appears that only the good and the very-best moments of times and people, stand out. My in-laws were good and loving, intelligent people – in particular, my father-in-law, Basil. They regarded and treated me very well and I regret the fact that I would eventually lose contact with them ... but life is not perfect. For a time, only for a brief moment, it appears to be so.

Even so, many good times abound and some of them happily survive the passage of the years. We settle into married life in a comfortable flat in a small, two-storey suburban block, where we share the upper floor with our landlords, the Zanniers: an Italian family who are to remain amongst my best friends over the ensuing fifty years. We live out-of-town at Coorparoo which, in these present times, would now be called inner-city. It is a friendly little community that we share. On the lower level of the flats, are two sets of young married couples and we all resonate happily together. One is an import-export agent for a wine distributer and thus, we have ready access to a regular supply of cheap bulk wines and occasionally enjoy some fine meals together.

The other couple, Russell and Dianne, are great fun. They are a picture-perfect couple – he, a handsome lifesaver and she, a pretty little blond 'stompy-wompy surfer girl', as the song of those times somewhat went. She and I share the same birthdate, right down to the very year. This marriage, in the long term, is to one day present a face of tragedy to Russell. They will have three model children, who will all assist their father in nursing their mother through a number of agonising years as she is slowly devoured by the cruel ravages of an all-consuming brain tumour. It is an ugly process and they are stalwart and resolute in their at-home caring and then their mother, his only love and my for a short time, 'star sister', is gone. The children set fine examples and Russell is so proud of the two daughters and his son. The son and one daughter have grown into world-class triathletes and on occasions, Russell proudly travels the world with them as they secure new victories for themselves out there. Then, on one very black day, not so very long after Dianne's departure from this life, the golden boy, Luke, is snatched up and taken away ... forever ... as he trains with his cycling team along a suburban road – taken by a woman driver with a long history of traffic infringements and misdemeanours. In an instant he is no more and Russell, still struggling to come to terms with the removal of the only love he ever found and dedicated himself to, now has the double impact of the loss of their only son, the shining one. The gods play with this man ... they grant him great financial success in his chosen line of business, they grant him prosperity, they grant him a sweet, petite and lovely partner in life and at the same time, take and take and take. Soon, he is to discover cancer lurking in the very chest which contains his own broken heart and along with all else, they demand one lung. And still he survives ... twenty five years later he is still hale, looking for all the world like some latter-day Burl Ives; strongly and confidently opinionated, as ever: a cheerful friend, in spite of his losses, not embittered but strong ... Heracles comes to mind in this instant.

For years, we maintain this exclusive ritual of gathering at each and every Christmas time ... called together by our once-landlord Ezzio, to relive and celebrate the genesis of our friendship. After fifty years of this, Ezzio, our charming perpetrator, is dead - gone, for something like three years now; himself, finally to the claims of his very-own lung cancer ... quietly, he went and ever so quietly, he continues to live on. His widow, our dear Domenica, Mrs Zann, through their daughter Lida, continues this celebration as Russell and I continue to be recalled every Christmas to repeat this ritual of a lifetime, with her and their daughter.

Lida herself, their perennial prodigal daughter, disappeared to her parents' homeland in Perugia; and from there sometime later, with her longterm partner Serge, to his hometown, Nice in France for altogether something like twenty-five years before finally returning home to her family. She and her father were, in essence so much alike as to cause them to clash in a fiery Mediterranean fashion at every turn throughout their tumultuous lives, right from her early teens when we first entered this family circle and until her eventual return - which was timely in enabling an end-of-days reconciliation, feisty though it may have continued to be, as Ezzio saw out his remaining years with us. She was a beautiful, intelligent girl, now grown into a mature woman with no loss of those attributes; always strongly-opinionated, she continues to rail against the rest of us - the feisty friend of a lifetime. She has a brother, Walter, slightly older who remained at home and did all of the right things by the family – gained a solid trade, took a wife, produced a modest family of offspring but ultimately, found himself on the receiving end of what became in time, a loveless marriage. An older man now himself, he continues his trade wrapped in the arms of a certain sadness and personal isolation.

* * * * *

AND SO, the married years make their way homewards. With marriage, the young gestating architect is saved from obscurity in an ammonia-laden drafting office when he finds comfort and respectability working for a good friend of his new in-laws – an office with a mix of architects and engineers, mostly engaged in designing for both new and existing hotels, racing clubs and related building types. The office sits in the central city fringes, just above street level, surrounded by windows and all of the city's bustle and he is given a level of design responsibilities rather than a simply mundane drafting role ... and respected for it without ever requesting the honour of this recognition. Life is looking good – and it is. In the evenings, he attends lectures at the university and often sits up late before the home drawing board developing his university design projects. He has not, as it turns out, paid a high price for his bout of the measles and aside from catching-up with the repeat subjects, his design component studies continue on course, on time – the repeat subjects do not really present a problem, having already been digested once. Life in the flat is balanced and contented; the couple's landlords and their downstairs neighbours all yield their share of pleasures in companionship; the newlyweds finally have a car and he now has a licence to drive it; friends and relatives on both sides of the marital table, all remain tangibly close-knit during this time; well before their own personal universes begin their inevitable expansions and outward drifts.

Modest in its trappings and expectations, life in this time of innocence is good – our own Golden Age, and most of us probably in those times, never looked very far beyond it. It appeared predictable and secure. This life would move forward and go where it was supposed to go; no nasty surprises, no tragedies, no betrayals ... the future, one long golden road.

My days (or rather, nights now) at university are drawing to their close. We have moved on from the flats and paid our modest deposit on a small but attractive, modest-sized cottage not far away in the same suburb – our first home. I can even now, feel its atmosphere inside and outside, particularly in the freshness of mornings for some reason ... and its then promise. I have finished my final year of design and all of the theory subjects. All that stands before me to finalise this course is the completion of my design thesis – which has managed to add one extra year to my six-year course. There is no real pressure bearing on me to create any overwhelming sense of urgency in this and so I work away, steadily researching my 'School of Performing Arts' as my chosen design thesis; in every spare moment, interviewing staff from my father-in-law's conservatorium of music and sitting for hours pouring over books both at home and in the city's public library, all the while writing down reams of notes – often mesmerising myself into an almost-asleep in the library, until it feels that there is no end to this process. And with this process my once bride, now wife, is often left at a loose end while I am absent, working in my head space both in and out of home ... and she drifts – until one day I find she has drifted so far with a supposed friend and fellow student, that there remains for me, no retrieving of her ... and if I am not in that instant already a cuckold, that condition is so close that it makes very little difference.

Eventually, I cannot ignore what sits before me; I confront her with the indisputable evidence and the choice she must make. We agree to separate. My thesis is yet to be finished but so too, has now become my relatively-young marriage. Being a mutually-agreed separation, at this time Australian law requires us to live out an interval of five years' separation to prove the breakdown's intractability. I myself, am in no hurry to charge down the path of matrimony again and I am patient to wait out this time. In a way, I see it as the granting of a default freedom, leaving me free to travel, (perhaps Japan, as I had once dreamed) to be my own agent – I will soon have my degree; no bonds and no ties. I will much later – years in fact – realise on looking back over my life that I had been not left entirely without some longterm scarring. At the time, my still-wife-in-name, views the situation differently, wishing to push by other means for a fast divorce so that she might quickly remarry ... before she is 'left on the shelf'? – at thirty? Many years later, I will realise that none of it was really so simple. Whilst not then consciously recognised by myself, the scars will sit deeply and the then-unacknowledged experience of deceit and final betrayal, probably tempers the unfinished course of many potentially-good and close relationships over the following years.

And so, life attends ... and so, it goes. She in time, will remarry to this person, bear him three children and then, when they have grown-up, she and the offspring will abruptly leave him one day – completely unforeseen by him. He in his turn, will be totally-devastated and seek counselling; and then, in a short time, will settle for setting up house with his own therapist ... karma? Where the wife takes herself at this point, remains to my ears, unknown. Life? ... who truly understands it?

The more news and current affairs programs that I witness these days, the bleaker seems to be our species' future ... or are they the same old stories, more insistently-presented? Have we always been in this spiral, most of us not noticing it for most of the time ... until it affects us – and we fail to make the connection?

* * * * *

SO, I AM CUT adrift. My in-laws appear to sympathise and their friend, my employer, when I inform him of our new separated status, shares his own observations with me, of the individual histories surrounding our marriage and confirms his absolute support for me in the matter. I am valued by the office and nothing changes for me at all in this workaday life. In this moment, I am not afforded the luxury of feeling sorry for myself and licking my wounds – word has come down the grapevine, without any formal notice being issued, that the university is clearing up the remnants of their 'old course', to make way for the students of the 'new course', whose years have now caught up with my own, being delayed as it was with my repeat subjects' year. The true impact of this is hammered home by the news that it is now the penultimate hour and I actually have no appreciable time at all left in which to complete my thesis. I contact Stan Kyle, our very proactive dean of the Faculty and explain my circumstances – 'the full catastrophe' as Zorba would so-dramatically have said. Stan responds accordingly and with empathy, securing one month's extension for me. This is very little time as I have not yet written one word (other than my copious collected notes) nor committed one drawn line to developing my design solution.

I am allowed to draw on one month of my holiday leave from the office. I retreat to the seclusion of my best man and his wife's home on the inner-city fringes at Bowen Hills. I vacate our onetime home, sell off the bulk of our furniture and place the property on the market. We have not been in possession of the house long enough to actually realise much gain on the sale but it has to be done. The location is good: it sells quickly and we divide the spoils equally before parting forever.

I lock myself away in my friends' room and get down to the business of completing this now-albatross of a thesis. For the next month, I live it day and night. At one point, I keep a record of my time and find that over one period of ten days, I manage to enjoy a total of twenty-four hours sleep. I stockpile a ream of newsprint (or butcher's paper) and start putting down ideas in words with bold felt pen on these large sheets. I start broadly, at the beginning: general subject breakdowns ... then chapters ... broad and loose. I tape these to the timber-lined walls of my room. Then I take each of these sheets and break it down further – chapters into sub-sections; sub-sections into basic elements; these into a summation of the information I've gleaned on each of them ... and so forth, until finally the walls of my cell are fully-papered – from floor to ten foot ceiling, with my thesis. All I have to do is connect the dots, sheet by sheet: write it all down and then come up with a building design.

My friend, Milan, has a photographic darkroom with an excellent enlarger, under their house and I use it to reproduce the illustrations accompanying my text and to copy my design drawings when they are complete; all with a wonderful camera film called 'micro-file', which makes for the sharpest and crispest of black-on-white images, to be reproduced finally on document paper. Meantime, I am proofreading the text which my typist is producing from my draft, correcting it and then again editing. One hundred and fifty pages later, I have a complete product in my hands to now be professionally bound in hard, cloth-finished volumes and soft-cover, copy versions. Amazingly, the task is completed in-toto with almost a week remaining to spare. Looking back, I still find it hard to believe that I managed to achieve this from start to finish in that time frame ... and, furthermore, that it is accepted by the faculty heads. I am done –

this long course of mine is finally complete. I have my degree and all that remains now is to gain my registration after a further twelve months of logged and certified office experience; along with the completion of the requisite written and oral examinations required by the Board of Architects. I can relax at last.

* * * * *

I SUPPOSE THAT for many of us, life might transpire in a fairly-ordered way from one day to the next, from one year to the next, from one state of affairs to a predictable-next ... employment, marriage, family, schools, empty nest, more families and on it advances in an orderly, expected file along life's super-highway – Zorba's 'The full catastrophe!'

Then one day, earlier for some, for others later ... it all can change, and that orderly procession then present a whole series of branching paths. When one is cut adrift as a solitary traveller (especially one having what is basically, an eclectic nature regarding overall interests in life, and having some small innate ability in many of them), the choices can often be misleading. But who is to say, with all the choices and the possible mistakes we might be induced, or seduced to make, what in the end was right or otherwise. After it is all done, there should be no looking back in anger or sorrow – no 'if-onlys', no regrets ... it was what it was ... and there, Edith Piaf, The Sparrow will always have it right on that account.

I carried away no visible baggage with me; at least none that I was ever conscious of or spoke about. I harboured no resentment, nor ever allowed any to possess me, in all of these years ... and I did wish my once-loved friends well. I embraced my new-found single state and found, or re-found, a host of new interests.

MY FATHER'S GHOST: A MEMOIR

And so, we are married, November 1968.

My new in-laws, Basil & Elsa, 'Hillhaven', Burleigh, 1970.

MY FATHER'S GHOST: A MEMOIR

Brisbane from New Farm clifftops, March 1972.

A family Christmas at Yeronga, 1971.
Bronwyn, Mum, Janis, Catriona, Jan's Robert, Dad & Glen

MY FATHER'S GHOST: A MEMOIR

Approaching the end of days, while a cyclone approaches.
Captain Cook Memorial Light, Point Danger, February 1972.

The Porpoise Pool at Snapper Rocks, Point Danger, February 1972.
The height of the cyclone and the slow winding-down of a marriage.

MY FATHER'S GHOST: A MEMOIR

Elephant Rock, beloved Currumbin, February 1972.
Our last holiday in a small beach-house opposite the Rock: stormy skies gathering.

7

Adrift & Alone in a New World

I CARRIED NO CLEAR VISION for where my future might now go. It was an open road and I, on it travelling alone. The only fixed goal was the finale of architectural registration in twelve months' time – and that presented no burden to my daily life. In the process of disposing our now mutually-unwanted furniture items, I happen to meet Estelle, a tall, attractive and somewhat older woman: a teacher and in similar circumstances – that of being separated; but accompanied by children of her own – and we form what is to be a short-lived relationship but one that restores what self-respect I may have lost during recent events and for a time, we are good for each other.

During this period, I find my way back into the theatre circle – which in itself, proves partly-instrumental in bringing about an end to my relationship with the teacher ... I am still very young and after my own marital implosion, it is all too much, too soon, to find myself as the potential subject of yet another connubial state – this, complete with half-grown children both anxious to replace their own father. In the face of brewing tensions, the decision to renew acquaintance with the theatre, sounds the death knell. We both know that the brushfire of the affair has quickly run its course and, just as quickly, expended itself – and with that, I move on into Brisbane's La Boîte Theatre to occupy my free moments away from the office.

Here, I make the acquaintance of Gary O'Neil and find myself casting for his production of 'Cactus Flower' to be staged at The Arts Theatre on Petrie Terrace. I am given role of Igor, the writer living next door to Toni, the Goldie Hawn character in the film: the much-younger girlfriend of the middle-aged dentist . The play and the film are one of those light he-loves, she-loves (while third parties complicate the plot) romantically-convoluted, at-cross-purpose comedies ... and as our rehearsals progress, so similar intrigues form amongst our cast; where 'she' throws herself shamelessly at 'him', never suspecting his true leanings; while the other 'he' is being led along by the other 'her'; meanwhile, the original 'he' is attempting to court the gormless second 'him'. None of this of course amounts to anything at the end of the day – except that the original 'he' does find a fitting love interest for himself via a late, minor-role addition to the cast and so they at least, get to live happily ever after. The subplot behind the scenes is perhaps more convoluted than the actual plot of the play.

This was once and for a long time, the essentially-harmless underscoring of much live theatre production. Rarely was anyone truly hurt or unduly compromised. As Robin Archer once prefixed her show (in 'Lola Blau', I believe it was), 'The theatre is life!' ... or something like that. In these now over-worked sanitised times, there would have been 'Me-too' arms being flung up from every corner of our cast with the hope for a moment's public glory splashed across the cover of Woman's Day or some such other scandal-laden weekly. Here, in more innocent times we flirt, we have our fun, no one takes offence and the play has a successful minor run.

With Cactus Flower behind us, I find myself happily settled in my new after-hours thespian home at La Boîte. The people are all warm, friendly and fun to be with. Jennifer Blocksidge, the theatre's director is welcoming. Gary has taken me on board as a friend and co-worker, taking me into his confidence as he casts around for another show to mount. He wants badly to do a musical and a little-known Australian number called 'Fetch Me A Fig-leaf' is on his want-to-do list. The show is set among the raunchy gods on Mount Olympus and contains some very catchy musical numbers ... but the cast is enormous and Gary is having difficulty in securing sufficient people of suitable caliber to mount it at this time, as many potential cast members are already committed to shows elsewhere (I have only now discovered in the archives, that Graeme Johnston – of our G&S's 'Patience' fame – did manage to produce the show at La Boîte during the following year, in July of 1974).

Gary rummages around for another show to stage and finally comes up with a small-cast Australian play by Mike Giles, named 'Rest and Recreation'. So, 'R&R' is powerful: a highly-charged drama, set mainly in the apartment of an Australian business couple based in Kuala Lumpur at the height of the Vietnam war. The husband encounters a pair of American servicemen in a bar, who are on R&R. He takes them home for the evening, where the younger proceeds to seduce the wife and trash their apartment. It is a powerful, primarily four-person drama: the husband, the wife, the senior American army officer and the younger. These four are played by Terri Whitehand (previously of the Ingrid Bergman role as the dentist's receptionist in 'Cactus Flower"), Barry Otto as the senior American (Barry is already a sound figure in Brisbane theatre and will secure for himself, an equally-sound future in Australian theatre and cinema, as one day, will his daughter Miranda), Peter Kowitz (a very-talented, young actor who will continue on to a solid future in both television and on the stage) and Ray Meagher (who at this time, hosts a late-night footy show and will eventually secure his easy-rolling, extremely-well-paid future playing Alf, forever and forever in television's 'Home and Away'). Terri turns in a well-balanced performance as the victimised wife; Ray plays her ever-so-wooden husband, whose talent for emoting consists of standing red-faced in one corner of the stage-in-the-round while his eyebrows perform amazing gyrations and other gymnastic feats to convey the turmoil inside, as his wife is slowly taken advantage of by these strangers; Barry presents a solid performance as the more balanced, mature but not truly in control, American senior officer; while Peter turns in an equally-solid performance as the junior Yank – his future as a promising actor is evident but so too is his youth, as his violent destruction of the couple's apartment lacks a certain level of discipline and control – and we are all grateful that the bottles and glasses on the bar-top are made of sugar and not the real thing, as fragments of them fly amongst the closest audience members each night.

My role initially is that of designer for the very minimal set and for the graphics of posters and programs. As the show progresses, I become enlisted for the, novel-for-myself, capacity of stage manager, due to the untimely unavailability for personal health reasons, of Maurine to the task. Suddenly, my role has greatly expanded from that of a rather static, one-off input, to a continuous responsibility from lights-up to lights-down, every night.

In a place like La Boîte in these early days, this is exciting, active and responsible and I greatly relish my task. Here then, at a late hour, comes into the scenario, as properties mistress, a bright young woman, Kathy. Props are relatively small for this show and so too, is the extent of her role – important as all roles are nevertheless. Between curtain-up and curtain-down (figuratively speaking that is, since as a theatre in the round we have no curtain – only lights), Kathy and I have a lot of time to spend together in the green rooms, as we monitor the show upstairs. We enjoy each other's company and without real design or intent, by the end of the show's run, we have fallen somewhat into each other's arms.

When I look back in later times, I will realise in one unexpected moment how very much she was like a young Natalie Wood before her tragic end. Before I know it, I am so totally lost in Kathy to such a powerful degree that she will continue to haunt me for some years to come ... it would seem, with no such reciprocal torments on her part. In the quiet moments between her sometimes very-late-night visits, I write poems for the first time ... to her ... and gauche as they might be (looking back through them now, I realise with some embarrassment, how much was drawn from some poets of that time, especially Rod McKuen whose love songs I, in my naiveté perhaps, imagined were all to women like my Kathy), I assemble them into a small bound volume with some drawn illustrations. One copy of this, I present to her, keeping the other for myself while she departs with her sister for England ... she, the high school science teacher, teaches me about gibbous moons, late night drives to the coast and how to wait patiently for her next appearance. I know that she also continues to date another but I endure that, in my state of absolute and total enchantment. It still seems complicated and I've never really understood it.

AT MY WINDOW

Gibbous moons
rise
full and yellow.
Occasionally,
when dust
is in the air,
red.
So too do
full moons,
half moons, like tonight.
If I were a fisherman
in the stars,
I would catch one
in a net of dreams
and lay it
at your door.

Lightning
when it storms,
spreads
in wondrous sheets
over its bed,
or falls
in deadly chains,
plunging,
striking,
causing you concern.
If I were a blacksmith
in the clouds,
I would collect them
and fashion in my forge,
necklaces of light
to place
around your neck.

Brad Drew © October 1973

She and her sister, Mary, have already planned their joint European adventure for the following year but I am unwilling to surrender her so easily. I had not planned such a move but in this moment, I decide that I will follow her across the globe to London and await her there, when she and Mary have done with their European odyssey and embarked on the English portion of their adventure. I am never to see her again. I do know what happens to her though – via a cousin of her father, whom I met when he visited the family during our all-too-brief affair. Bill lives in England's Market Harborough, in Leicestershire, and will maintain a casual friendship with me during my time in England ... and in so doing, keep me updated regarding her life. She will eventually meet and marry a chartered accountant from Scarborough in the north and settle with him back in Australia, where she will proceed to make babies and in all likelihood, never return to high school science teaching.

* * * * *

AND SO, THIS NEW DIE IS CAST ... life suddenly assumes a new direction and I am to be London-bound. During this thespian year post-thesis, I have returned to my roots in a sense. I have taken a flat in that very same terrace house block on Coronation Drive: the 'Home Flats', where I spent my first two years of life ... this time, I am in a large ground floor flat, at the corner fronting the Drive and Park Road. Park Road in the current time, has long been a busy and popular neighbourhood centre with an emphasis on trendy eateries; and my flat on the corner, at last sighting, has become a very upmarket restaurant. I have lived theatrically in this flat for most of the year. It is central, relatively handy to my office and close by La Boîte. With the blessing of the landlords, I have repainted its rather old world interior, matt black with tones of white to its classical arch and columns dividing the space and throughout its upper reaches; white low-set vinyl upholstery with large, suspended cardboard tubes encased in beaten silver as improvised suspended downlighting (alfoil crumpled, then smoothed out and glued) with matching silver beaten over the panelled doors, to complete the scene ... all very dramatic and a favourite haunt for post-theatre parties. It is here that the 1974 Brisbane flood is lived through.

On the eve of the great inundation, we are all enjoying a cast party in an apartment overlooking Main Street at Kangaroo Point (I believe it belonged to Eileen Beatson, a charming and delightful Englishwoman: a major figure and director at La Boîte through these years, who introduces me that evening, to the wonderfully-English Gin and Roses). The rain starts up and a cyclone warning is issued over the radio; the atmosphere is fast building into what is going to be some very-nasty weather. In dribs and drabs, we all suddenly rush away from our celebrations. Gary O'Neil, our director, lives with his parents at Wynnum, a considerable distance away and so, I offer my nearby flat for the evening and there, we hastily retreat. Come morning, we are stranded at the terrace houses – cut-off and isolated. It seems we are fortunate to be placed on a piece of high ground, there in the heritage flats. Coronation Drive, following the riverfront, is cut off by water a short distance in each direction and likewise, Park Road itself is cut off at its intersection with Milton Road, underneath the railway bridge. We are on an island but safely high and dry.

We are to be castaways here for the following week or more. The electricity is off for the interim but we do have town gas for cooking and heating water ... and we do still have our water supply. The landlords live in the flat behind mine and between us, we have a reasonable supply of non-perishable foodstuffs with which we manage to improvise quite decent shared meals. With no hot water supply working, we pull out a large boiler to mount on the gas stove and with it prepare a warm bath which, after the latter-day style of 'The Young Ones' household, we take turns in using – although no bicycles are to be found under the remaining sludge ... it's not much but we manage to keep ourselves fairly fresh at least. We have between us, one battery-powered radio with which to keep track of the outside world and deliverance from our imposed isolation; and we spend our evenings together, playing cards by candlelight. Our spirits are bolstered, quite literally, by making joint excursions along to the Royal Exchange Hotel at Toowong to replenish our good cheer. We manage this on the high, dry ground by climbing up the embankment at the railway overpass at Milton Road and then, by walking along the now-silent railway lines to our destination at Toowong, alongside the station there. We stock up on comfort fluids and retrace our steps homewards with our booty. At the height of the flood, the water police come by on dusk to warn us of the impending wall of water due to approach us at midnight and they ask if we want to jump ship, to be rescued from it. Reasoning that if this is likely, then far better we stay in order to move our most valuable items to one of the upstairs flats, we refuse their offer. As midnight approaches, we line the footpath frontage of the building to view the approaching 'tsunami'. When it does come, all that it can manage is to wash across Coronation Drive and lap against the lower steps leading from the footpath up to the front doors: a height difference of some further 1.5 to 2.0 metres up to the ground floor where we live. This proves in that moment, to be something of an anticlimax and we resume our Robinson Crusoe lives here until the waters finally recede, allowing us to drive out into the broader world again.

    At this time, Kathy and her sister are already in Europe and miss out on this drama of the great flood; which will be all but lost to the vaults of history by the time the next such inundation arrives – at which time when people will beat their breasts ever more-strenuously, cast around for a human focus of blame and demand more restitution from someone, anyone; it will seem as if this flood of 1974 never happened (nor the equivalent one of 1893, for that matter). In these current times, whatever might happen today or yesterday is presented as the worst of its kind that has ever transpired – our sense of history now retains a very short memory.

My parents' home at Yeronga does not fare so well ... it is fortunate and an aspect to be grateful for, that its internal construction is of single-skinned T&G pine boarding and it is elevated beneath its floor level; for at the height of the flood it is embraced by water through it, almost to the joinery head; this happens in spite of being half a metre above ground level at the front and over two metres above at the back. It is also fortunate that Dad knows his way around electricity, for at the height of the flood he swims through the house, turning off lights and appliances such as the kitchen refrigerator – which continues to chug its merry way underwater, with its door seals so tight that no water ever enters it. In the many years afterwards, the family continues to use this plucky beast as their second refrigerator in their succeeding homes. After the waters finally recede, a great community spirit rises up as friends and neighbours assist each other with the cleanup of the sludge which now coats everything – sweeping, mopping and hosing all evidence away. Many of my beloved childhood books which had remained at home, are lost and I recall the sad day when we hauled out our poor, doomed piano onto the front footpath ... its keys had swollen so enormously that they resembled a rolling, roiling wave with all of their ivories popped off and sitting loosely on the surface of the keys; its iron sounding frame and strings, now a brown mass of new rust; its veneers warped and lifting – nothing is left to be done but to break it up piece by piece, with sledgehammers, into scarcely-recognisable pieces to be taken away by the Council's kerbside collection trucks at day's end: an ignominious end to a fine, if modest, instrument. People generally, did not create a great hubbub of publicised noise over any of this process – they cleaned up the mess, if sadly, and got back on with their lives. It would probably never be quite the same again for many but they bore it, in the main, quietly. Mum felt that the house never quite smelt the same afterwards; that the smell of the silt remained trapped within the joints of the walling … and eventually, while I was overseas, they would sell up Yeronga and buy themselves a new home: brick-veneer, on high ground, in Brisbane's Mt Gravatt – and be the fortunate recipients of another piano: an old pianola, passed on to them by a good old friend.

* * * * *

IN THE MEANTIME, it is fast-approaching April and the turning-over point towards a new life in London. In my youthful, cast-adrift-on-the-sea-of-life exuberance and rejuvenated theatre involvement, I naively imagine a romantic vision of this move being forever. I am following Kathy, with the less than realistic notion that somehow we will pick up from where we left off and in the meantime, I shall pursue a career on the London stage, eventually yielding up architecture along the way. Meanwhile, I shall have to support myself somehow, since I haven't set myself enough time to put much in the way of funds away for this impromptu venture; and so, before departing the security of home, I have contacted a professional recruitment company in London to prepare for architectural employment. I have divided my still-scant possessions into what to take, including my music collection, to my new life and what to store back here with my family; I have my passport and ticket and the princely sum of two thousand dollars in travellers' cheques; and finally, I arrange for my required inoculations ... administered after a fine dinner one evening with a good doctor friend and his wife: one of my former wife's employers, with both of whom I continue to remain friendly. I shall much later, again stumble across the pair of these paediatric surgeons with their wives, one Saturday morning in London, as we all coincidentally step off the tube together at South Kensington. One learns that the world can sometimes be a very small place.

After receiving these shots for my trip (and having stepped on a rusty drawing pin earlier that day), I wake in the small hours of that morning racked by the most violent and uncontrollable shivering and, forgetting that one of the shots was for malaria, in the dullness of interrupted sleep, I imagine that I am dying of tetanus and dramatically burst into quiet tears with visions of my Czech friends, with whom I am again staying in my final days of Brisbane, finding me dead in my bed when they rise in the morning. Oh, the drama – Oh, the unjust tragedy! ... Come morning, I am still alive.

Come evening later that day (having finished up my last day at the office and taking farewells with my co-workers at our local hotel), I visit my Italian friend Lida, from the early marriage years, to say my goodbyes to her where she now lives locally with her paramour. Now, it is her turn to imagine that I am dying ... this time, by her hand. The two of them have been smoking a little grass (as one did in those times – today that seems tame from within the current 'Ice' epidemic). I have consumed a modest amount of red wine with my work-fellows at the office and Lida now prepares a three-paper reefer to share with me on my arrival. Not being used to any significant amount of the substance myself and being left to consume most of this generous offering alone, I find myself unbelievably, horribly sick and pass out draped across their bed after exiting the ensuite. There Lida finds me, prone, ashen, motionless and believes in this moment that she has killed me in some overtly-Shakespearean fashion ... Once again, I manage to live.

    This is how I spend my last days in Brisbane. My final night is spent packing, weighing, discarding and repacking, as I seek to reduce my suitcase to twenty kilograms (I have already sent one identical suitcase on ahead, by air freight to be collected later in London). Finally, somewhere around two in the morning, I get the balance right and grab a few hours sleep before rising for my morning flight. Milan and Sue provide me with an excellent bottle of champagne with which to while my initial flight away. I check in and board my flight – and we are up and off to Singapore, my stopover for four days, before continuing on to Gatwick via a brief set-down in Bahrain, where the tarmac swarms with sullen, camouflage-clad soldiers, bearing submachine guns: just a tad unnerving for that brief moment.

> The wise among us shun love
> Green fields and distant skies.
> The wise live and breathe each day
> As the cow chews her endless cud.
> Their ways are simple and direct
> And their lives
> Tick steadily around the clock
> Toward the same inevitable end.
> But then
> The wise have never loved.

Brad Drew © January 1974

MY FATHER'S GHOST: A MEMOIR

Cook Terrace, Coronation Drive, Milton in 1973.
Designated a World Heritage Site in October, 1992.

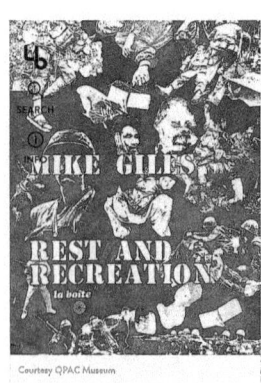

Courtesy QPAC Museum

REST AND RECREATION
September 21st, 1973 — October 13th, 1973

VENUE

La Boite Theatre, Brisbane

PRODUCER	CAST	SET DESIGNER
La Boite Theatre	Ray Meagher	Brad Drew
	Julie Long	
DIRECTOR	Barry Otto	**LIGHTING DESIGNER**
Gary O'Neil	Peter Kowitz	Chris Harmston
	Terry Whitehand	
PLAYWRIGHT	Leone Hendry	**SOUND DESIGNER**
Mike Giles		Alan Ball

My program & poster artwork for Mike Giles' 'Rest and Recreation';
At Brisbane's La Boite Theatre in September 1973.

My flat at Cook Terrace through later 1973 is Ground Floor left.
My earliest childhood years spent in First Floor flat at rear of this.

Inside Cook Terrace: a favoured cast-party venue – high drama.
It is here, that we sit out the 1974 Brisbane floods.

Kathy, who drew me to London, at her family home, Oxley, in 1973.

8

Singapore & Onwards towards London

WE SET DOWN IN SINGAPORE. Here, I will spend the next three days; first, purchasing a new camera along with a large complement of lenses, filters, carry-case and tripod, before setting out to explore this immaculate, incredibly-clean city ... this is 1974 and even in this time, there exist very stiff fines for littering: in the order of $500 Singapore on the spot, for as much as dropping a cigaret butt or a wad of gum – in consequence, the city is spotless.

I am stopping over in a large modern hotel named the Ming Court, with all the trappings for the tourist visitor, sitting as it does in Tanglin Road at the edge of the tourist belt. It would be dwarfed by the Singapore of the present time but in 1974, with its 350 rooms built only four years earlier and its style modelled in a token fashion after the glories of China's Ming Dynasty, it represents the height of luxury for this guileless young traveller ... and it is budget priced as part of my total airline package to London. I was never fond of the humid heat of summers back home but that memory pales beside the tropical conditions here. On my first morning, I am collected by my taxi driver attached to the hotel, who seems to have assigned himself solely to me and he takes me to the recommended shopping outlets for my photographic shopping venture; where he waits for me (as he does each day that I am here, driving me to where I ask and waiting to take me on to my next stop, wherever that might be ... all for an amazingly small amount of money for the full day's engagement, by Australian terms) and then returns me to the hotel until I need him again. Up in my spacious air-conditioned room, I excitedly unpack my purchases, load my camera with film and step out onto my private balcony to take my first photos of the city. Instantly, after the cool dry atmosphere of the room inside, both viewfinder and lens fog up – completely; such is the climate of this place. In the evening, up in the rooftop garden of the hotel, I discover the culinary delights of Malaysian satay. It is inexpensive and delicious. For a novice traveller with, at this stage, limited experience of the world's foodstuffs, it is both exotic and addictive ... for the remainder of my stay here, I eat little else for lunch or for the evening meal.

  The following day, I set off to take in some of the local sights, ferried around with care and attention by my faithful driver, our first stop being the Tiger Balm Gardens: a multitiered meandering garden filled with sometimes-gruesome, painted concrete sculptures drawn from an expansive selection of Eastern mythology and folklore – confusing perhaps but impressive. Singapore is full of novelty gardens and so, we move on from here to The Bird Gardens: a vast park where distances can be reduced by riding a trackless train of small carriages running on wheels with tyres, towed by a small vehicle. It is here, on one of these whistle-stops, that I am befriended by a charming old Anglo-Indian lady, a Mrs Radoo. She is the senior member of a larger family group headed up by Mr Tom Bond, an Englishman from Portsmouth. His wife came originally from Malaysia and is a midwife, while their two daughters are both nurses. They are a lively, warm and friendly group and they adopt me as a de-facto son for the remainder of my stay here – or so Tom tells me when he says I must write my own father and reassure him that I am in good hands.

He tells me that I must visit them for a weekend when I am finally settled in London – and this, I eventually do. At some point, they suggest that I release my driver for the rest of the day and join them, as we all move on to the Japanese Gardens for afternoon tea – and then later, it's back to their own apartment for dinner (receiving my first instruction in the use of chopsticks in the process); after which they show me the sights of Singapore's Night Market in Bugis Street, filled with noise and lights, crowds and a host of new and exotic street-food. Mrs Radoo sees me safely home to my lodgings afterwards. Looking back on all of this unsolicited behaviour: of being semi-adopted and taken care of by kind strangers in strange places, I realise how very innocent I was at twenty-five and how comparatively so, the wide world then was – how much, in our fresh and innocent greenness, we took on trust in those safe and trustworthy times.

* * * * *

AS QUICKLY AS IT SEEMS to have begun, my time in Singapore is suddenly over and I am on my way to board the British Caledonian flight to my new home. I had arrived here on a British Airways flight – tourist class of course but sheer luxury compared with the somewhat smaller charter flight aircraft which we are now boarding. I have thought myself clever in managing to be allocated a window seat (one of the few remaining ones, in Row 13; so of course, most people have avoided taking it) ... a feat I am soon to regret.

There are three seats on each side of the central aisle. I am seated early and watch the parade of assorted travellers now boarding with the most alarming collection of cabin baggage – including a pair of surfing addicts, replete with their surfboards even, which they attempt to somehow stow away in the overhead lockers. My companion, now sitting in our central seat, is an ancient Cambodian grandmother travelling to join her family in Paris, along with her late-teenage grandson, who occupies the aisle seat. He is smartly-dressed in a western suit and speaks English fluently, whilst she is well-and-truly traditional in her all-black, loose pyjama suit; and naturally, speaks no English – French perhaps but English, no. She carries in with her, a very large basket of ripening mangoes and a smaller, second basket with hinged lid and compartments containing her betel nut ingredients ... plus a collection of Chinese movie magazines. All of these accoutrements descend to the limited floor space where they spill themselves outwards, pinning my feet against the window wall while she removes her sandals and places her feet, cross-legged across her lap, selects a magazine and enters the complex ritual of preparing her betel nut melange ... pink paste spread over green leaf, sprinkle with shredded brown leaf (not unlike tobacco), roll the lot and partially slice with a special hinged cutter ... finally, chews contentedly with a big smile and, while the plane prepares to taxi for take-off (she ignores the seatbelt, mind you), spits the rose-coloured leftovers into a paper doggy-bag. Meantime, she cannot help herself leaning across me with an engaging pink grin as she takes in the view from the window and shares her movie stars with me.

I am not sure that I can endure the next crammed fourteen hours in-flight like this. With my own winning smile, I lean across to her grandson and engage him in conversation, suggesting to him that his grand-mere might better enjoy having the window seat with its view? He relays this to her and she radiates instant joy. So, we do the seat shuffle ... she is ecstatic, he is happy to occupy her vacated seat and I take his, on the aisle, where I find that there is a bonus afforded in this move; with the extra leg-space of the aisle when no-one is travelling down it.

We have only one set-down between here and London ... in Bahrain. When we land there, we have a half-hour stopover while the aircraft is cleaned, refuelled and replenished with meals. We are removed from the plane, to then walk across the open tarmac (sprinkled with sullen, armed soldiers toting sub-machine guns) to the terminal while this happens. Leaving the aircraft is like entering a vast oven – the heat is tremendous; its only saving grace is that it is dry, and as such, amazingly tolerable. Finally, we return to our craft. In the seats directly in front of me, sit a young woman with her small daughter who are joining her German husband, an engineer, in Paris. We had chatted for a time, back in the terminal, before departure.

These in-flight events could never happen in the present time, in the light of post-millennium history ... at some point into the flight, the hostess asks the young mother if her little girl would like to spend some time up front in the cockpit – which they happily elect to do, much to my envy. A little later, the same hostess manages to spill hot coffee on me as she serves. I take this opportunity to ask her if I might also spend some time up front. She checks with the pilot, who gives his approval; after the girl and mother have returned. Thus, I enjoy the privilege of spending around half-an-hour, up there behind the pilot, while he explains his array of instruments and dials, as we pursue the fleeting sunset across Europe; the mountains of Turkey glowing purple below us in the day's last light, as pinspots of lights turn on over the slopes and in the valleys between. It is a magical moment and I am fortunate to have enjoyed it.

Finally, we approach our late-evening, darkened landfall at Gatwick Airport: London's second airport after Heathrow. Due to a strong headwind, we have lost precious time in arriving here and, by the time I have been cleared through immigration and arrived at customs, it is close to midnight. I must look the gauche young innocent as I approach the customs desk and stand waiting, with my collection of baggage both hanging off my shoulders and gripped in both hands. The bearded customs officer in his peaked cap, looking for all the world the part of an old sea captain, straight out of some literary work, finally looks up at me and says, 'Well, laddie ... what do you want then?'

To which I reply, 'Don't you want to look through my bags?'

His response to this is, 'You don't have anything you shouldn't have in there, do you?'

My reply, is a questioning, 'No?'

'Well, be off with you then,' is his rejoinder.

By this time, I am the only non-staff person remaining in the airport terminal; and there are very few staff remaining either. I remember Gatwick in those moments, as being a vast and lofty, coldly-echoing hall with many of its surfaces including walls, tiled and with an overall feeling of art deco style about the place. This was some fifty-plus years ago – I have never seen it again and so my memory could be flawed.

In any case, it is now sometime after midnight, in a strange country with no idea at all of where I am in relation to London (or anywhere else); this echoing mausoleum where I find myself is almost deserted and there is no sign of Billy, who was to meet my flight and take me back to Market Harborough. I find a public noticeboard displaying a short note from him, explaining how, with such lateness of the hour, he has had to return home or miss his last train and be also, stranded. He leaves his telephone number with an instruction to call him in the morning, for directions on how to find my way to Leicestershire and Market Harborough, where he will meet me.

Fine ... but what do I do tonight? I manage to find one counter, still with a staff member at this late hour, who arranges a private taxi to take me to a hotel-motel nearby, where he assures me I will find accomodation for the night. My first views of this green England follow, as we drive along dark, overhung lanes, seemingly little wider than the small sedan itself, bounded by high, tidy drystone walls and hedges, with the occasional hare darting across the glare of the headlamps. Finally, after about twenty minutes, we arrive in the middle of the countryside, at my refuge, for what remains of the night: the Copthorne Hotel. A porter carries the bulk of my luggage ahead of me, as he escorts me up to my room. Tired and feeling dearly in need of a shower after the long flight on such a very-crowded aeroplane, what greets me at this hour seems nothing short of absolute luxury: I have a double room, with a cosy bathroom, a very-large, curtained bath and the most wonderful hot, hot, hot shower. Late as it is, I must rejuvenate myself under its high-pressured, steaming stream for an extended and invigorating, oh-so-gratefully-felt eternity; before at last, crawling thankfully into bed. Aah, the sheer bliss! I am here at last; I am safe, clean, warm; and the bed is spacious, crisp and comfortable. All else will be fine in the morning. My new life has begun.

* * * * *

COME DAWN, after a small sleep-in and a late breakfast, I am ready to face my new day: the first day of a brave new life. I breakfast simply at the hotel and phone Billy to receive my directions. I collect my luggage from the room, engage my private taxi and head back to

MY FATHER'S GHOST: A MEMOIR

Gatwick to restart the adventure, all over again. I carry one large rigid-polypropylene suitcase, a leather case not unlike a Gladstone bag in shape, size and proportion, a canvas shoulder bag, my everyday man-bag, my new camera case with separate tripod case and an umbrella. With this collection of albatrosses hanging from and gripped about my person, I set off as instructed, onto the underground connection line as far as London's Kings' Cross-St Pancras. With my arthouse silver jewellery biting into my fingers under the pressure of my various burdens, I lug all this personal luggage along with me, working my way through the labyrinthine bowels of the tube system and then, across the roadway which separates Kings' Cross from St Pancras, and onto the British Rail overground train which will carry me at last to my place of recovery for the next two weeks; with Billy at his Market Harborough.

Thankfully, there he is, patiently awaiting me. Once there, he takes me back with him to homely comfort, my own warm welcoming bedroom and a hearty, freshly-made meal. I am exhausted and by now, entering a level of jet-lag but this is so good: such a nurturing refuge at the end of my long journey.

I catch up on the latest travel news of Kathy and Mary, which contains little to hearten me greatly, with respect to a future together with her; but it does remain a remnant of a dream, to which I continue to cling, albeit tenuously. Over the coming week or two, I am introduced to Bill's friendly village: a small, picturesque township of assorted historical Midlands styles with a number of Georgian residences scattered through and with a small, elevated, Tudor grammar school sitting at its centre, having an arched open market place beneath. We take our easy time, walking its length and breadth, meeting his friends and neighbours, while I enjoy my first introductions to small English pubs. The people are without exception, warm and friendly, and I am made to feel quite at home.

This makes for a comfortable recovery from the last, long leg of my journey and makes for a perfect welcome to the English way of life. I feel immediately that I am going to be at home here ... from this modest start, there comes a strong sense of instant belonging.

MY FATHER'S GHOST: A MEMOIR

Singapore from my room at the Ming Court Hotel, April 1974.

Parish Church, Old Grammar School & Square, Market Harborough, 1974.

9

London at last

SOON IT IS TIME TO MOVE ON, and into London properly. I shall continue to remain in touch with Bill who will occasionally visit me in the city. Gathering my overwhelming collection of luggage about my person, I head off once again, retracing my steps back to St Pancras and there, across the road to the underground at King's Cross: a collection point for six Underground lines, one of which will deliver me to my destination. At this point, the burden of my cumbersome luggage is wearing very thin and in a moment of weakness, I opt to transfer it all, with myself, into the nearest traditional 'black cab'. This proves a good move for I now get an excellent view, travelling overground through my new home ... it is novel, exciting and different. There is such a pervading sense of age and condensed, embodied history everywhere I look. I have no idea of where we might be at any point, nor where we might be going, but I am simply caught up in the novelty and freshness of it.

Before I had left home, Stan Marquis-Kyle, the dean of our architecture faculty had given me sound, almost-fatherly advice on where to initially stay upon reaching London. He had himself, spent a large part of the previous year of his sabbatical in London and had made a very good friend of the owner of a modest private hotel there – where both he and the owner had each purchased kits for constructing clavichords and afterwards had remained in touch. The Morton Court Hotel in Courtfield Gardens is owned and run by Richard Groves and his wife. Stan has prepared them for my arrival and I am made generously at home from the outset ... and at a very modest weekly cost. The hotel is only a short walk from Earl's Court station, in the heart of what at this time is known (embarrassingly to the please-don't-call-me-ocker snob in me) as Kangaroo Valley ... no matter.

In our current time, Mister Google shows me that very little has changed here at Morton Court, inside or outside (apart from paintwork, furnishings and the general amenity of rooms which have been upgraded into the expectations of travellers in the twenty-first century – the exterior to all purposes, unchanged), except for ownership. It is now quite fashionably known as 'The Nadler Kensington' but even so, I still recognise the corridors and stairwells as if it were only yesterday ... the dining room has disappeared and the rooms are all equiped with their own smart ensuites, while new artwork adorns the once-dim, now-bright hallways. In my own time, it is very much occupied, in the main, by longterm residents, mostly demure middle-aged matrons. There is an old-fashioned, almost

Dickensian quality to the place which sadly, does also extend to most of the output from the kitchen: breakfast bacon, pallid and limp alongside uninspired just-fried eggs; similarly-anaemic gammon slices with potato mash and overcooked cabbage in the evenings. The dining room is friendly but gently-bathed in a certain quietly-polite sobriety. The Groves are easygoing, intelligent and accept me into the embrace of the hotel as yet another family member. I am always welcome in their large but cluttered private office and Richard often invites me to accompany him when he visits his fraternity of other hotel owners in the area.

On one of these visits, to celebrate the opening of a neighbour's new private bar, I am startled to hear my name called out questioningly, as I cross the foyer floor ... there, sitting behind the reception counter is Barbara, (away from whom I had sprinted back over the fence to home, in that now-distant night following her school formal). I have not seen her in all of these intervening years and now, here she is, having been working at this post for some time ... and what is more, her father Earl (he of the many attempts to gain progeny other than daughters) is in town and right now, is occupying the very bar party to which Richard and I are headed. Later that year, as my friends and I embark on our coach tour of the West Country, I will discover Earl's wife, in the act of boarding the neighbouring coach, bound for Scotland. This type of coincidence will follow me through all my years in London. I am to be constantly amazed at how one can cross over to the other side of the world, all the way to London, and encounter time and again, people from a past age, who might never have been encountered by chance back home.

* * * * *

SLOWLY, I BEGIN to acquaint myself with my splendid new world. Short forays from the safety of my Morton Court refuge at first. Little by little, I determine what lies about me. Shortly, on one Friday, I travel to Heathrow Airport to collect my other case of belongings, which I had sent ahead as freight and once there, I am overwhelmed by the vastness of the terminal. Roughly six weeks will pass before I finally contact the employment agency to inform them of my arrival and even longer time passes before I secure accomodation of my own. In the interim, I explore and come to terms with what I have done, dropping myself into this wonderful city. I discover there are two publications essential to living in London ... first and most important for finding one's way around, is the paperback-sized 'London A-Z'; and second, is the 'Time Out' weekly magazine which contains page after page of information allowing one to access every cultural activity worth pursuing: theatre of every type and classification, from West End to provincial; cinema along similar lines; art shows and special exhibitions ... there is no end to the listings.

One balmy Sunday afternoon, I take myself to explore Hyde Park and Kensington Gardens for the first time. I discover that it is comfortably reached on foot from where I am staying; as with time I find, is so very, very much of central London. It is still April and a sunny spring day, and as I walk through this iconic green heart of the city, I am astonished to observe what the supposedly-staid and proper English do when the sun shines, after the deprivations of winter ... they flock into parks and gardens everywhere and remove most of their clothing. There, before me, spread about the lawns and recumbent on deckchairs are people, old and middle-aged people even, in their underclothes; matronly bodies, pale, strapped into white corsets, camisoles or step-ins like my mother wore, reclining like so many beached white whales along a distant foreign shoreline. There is no end to the surprises that London will hold for me over the coming years.

* * * * *

Redcliffe Gardens & ventures into Questors

I HAD KNOWN JANE Atkins for a short time at La Boîte, before she and her mother, 'Mrs A', left for London. Jane is a very-talented actress and aspiring theatre director and she has come here to further her dream. They are well entrenched in London by the time I arrive, along with their dear friend Maurine, whom I had replaced as stage manager for the production of 'R & R'; at that time, for her own health reasons. She also, has transferred her life to London: the world's theatrical nexus. During my settling-in period, I have located Jane, 'Mrs A' and Maurine, comfortably settled in Redcliffe Gardens, a comfortable walk down the road from where I am currently living.

The house at 82 Redcliffe Gardens is one door removed from Redcliffe Gardens Square and is a charming residential address – there is an elevated ground floor with a sub-basement level opening into a lovely private garden in back; above this are two spacious floors, each of which houses two self-contained comfortable flats: one streetside, one overlooking the rear garden; finally at top, within the slate-clad mansard roof-space, is a charming lone flat ... this is where my trio of theatrical friends live. It is cosy and comfortable ... and, so far above the ground level, quiet. Presiding over all this, is the petite and likewise-charming Mrs Moysey: the owner and landlady whose home, with her late husband, it had been through the long years of WW2.

She had once been a ballet dancer, and a very pretty one at that; as remains in evidence, even now. She maintains a happy and comfortable household and displays an obvious liking for younger male company – with the exception of the Atkins household in the roof space, the other flats are all occupied by men, all younger than her of course. There are also a number of old friends, also male, who often visit. One of her theatrical friends provides her with a steady flow of theatre tickets, from which we often benefit; she is at that age when one seldom ventures forth at night and so, many gifted tickets are passed on to us.

Thus provided for from the outset, I commence my theatre feasting with Lindsay Kemp's production of 'Flowers' at the Collegiate Theatre (later to be renamed the Bloomsbury Theatre); to be followed by 'Don Giovanni' at Covent Garden and 'The Rocky Horror Show', at the King's Road Theatre. So impressed am I by 'Flowers', that I take myself off to see it again the following week ... for myself at this time, it embodies the heart and soul of the art of the theatre: drama, pathos, dance and mime, with almost no spoken dialogue at all. It is pure and simply 'theatre', stripped to the bone. I will attend this show many times over the succeeding years in other locations (including Brisbane in the years following my eventual return there), along with whatever other productions of Lindsay Kemp's company that I can find; including 'Salome' and 'Mr Punch's Pantomime'. Notables such as David Bowie and Kate Bush owed much to his teaching and mentoring, and even now I continue to revere his memory and craft.

At Redcliffe Gardens, we are all fired up to tackle our own craft of the theatre. In the time since she arrived in London, Jane has attended a course in television direction and production, whilst working for a firm of solicitors in the Inns of Court, in Lincoln's Inn Fields near Holborn tube station. This is still a time of random bombings by the IRA and of sudden blackouts, due to the coal miners' strikes through the early 1970s. Here in Jane's office, they often find themselves working through their day by candlelight and quite often we find ourselves climbing the spiralling stairs forever, up out of the bowels of the very-deep Holborn tube station, when the lifts' power has been cut; and passing older citizens, slumped red-faced against the curving, riveted steel wall, gasping to recover their breath at around the halfway ascension point. In a very short time, one adapts and learns to live with these inconveniences and the threat of the occasional bomb comes to be regarded with a fairly-blasé attitude – what can one do? Life goes on and the reminders of these events are few and random.

We at Number Eighty-two meanwhile, prepare to make a serious foray into the world of the theatre. Jane considers that the Questors Theatre at Ealing will be a good place to start. I have already studied the theatre building here, as being a newly-built, groundbreaking adaptable facility, while I was preparing my thesis. We enlist and are introduced to their Studio Theatre facility, as Jane prepares us to produce our 'shop window'; which will share the evening's presentation with two other short plays. We elect to produce a playlet by the name of 'Johnson', taken from Paul Ableman's collection of surreal short plays called 'Tests'. It is an absurd piece in the tradition of Becket and Ionesco, featuring three players: myself, a doctor from the Brompton Chest Hospital named David Girling, and a Ken Ratcliffe ... and with no set, nor costumes as such. Some time later in this same year, David will reappear in another shop window produced by Jane – in a two-man play, 'The Architect and the Emperor of Assyria' by the Spanish playwright Arrabal; for this, I shall design the set, program and props (including a sizeable collection of soldered wire masks, made by myself during our chilly November evenings, back at my flat after the architectural working day). This will be a more substantial piece of theatre, presented to a larger audience.

* * * * *

CPB & The Barbican

WHILE 'JOHNSON' IS IN PREPARATION, I finally take myself off to my employment agency to apply for work. The timing is perfect and I am directed to the esteemed offices of Chamberlin Powell and Bon, who are the architects for the Barbican Redevelopment, just north of St Paul's Cathedral. At CPB, I am interviewed and happily taken into their fold on a contract basis. Here, I am destined to remain over the next three years, until my eventual return home. In less than a year, the office will invite me to join their full-time staff (there is an advantage for them in this of course: they no longer have to pay the agency's regular commission and, while the step does involve a cut in my take-home weekly pay, I do now get holiday pay and public holidays) ... they are obviously comfortable with me and happy with my work. When I join the office, the Barbican project has entered into its final stages: that of the Arts Centre. Architecturally, the work is exciting and the office is rich and varied, hardworking but friendly, warm and fun.

The Barbican is a very old area of London (the walled area of the Old Fort dating from around 200AD) which was heavily laid waste by the bombings of WW2 ... and it mostly sat that way until the end of the 1950s, when the Corporation of the City of London called for a competition to reclaim this lost heart. The three friends who would drive this project to its completion were originally, each of them, occupied in academic contexts and only came together to form the practice when one of them won the competition for a large residential project, Great Arthur House in the Golden Lane Estate, close to the Barbican at the beginning of the fifties. They cut their teeth as a practice on this commission and in 1954, were invited to submit designs for the redevelopment of the lost Barbican itself. Three designs were submitted from 1955 to the final design in 1959. This eventual design would serve to heavily sustain the now-large practice from this time forward until 1984, when the Arts Centre is finally completed.

During this time, Geoffrey Powell will maintain a separate office at Little Britain near Aldersgate, working on the practice's other projects, while the overall design core and detailing coordination of the Barbican will be administered by Peter 'Joe' Chamberlin and Christoph Bon from their large offices at Lamont Road, in Chelsea; and, where I find myself, in the day-to-day working heart of the project, located at Sydney Mews in South Kensington – within easy walking distance up the Fulham Road from their Chelsea office.

The Barbican is vast, housing maisonettes and flats in low-rise, crisscrossing ribbons of blocks up to seven stories high; along with tall, slender tower blocks of apartments (at the time, these were the tallest residential towers in Europe); a percentage of ground-level commercial tenancies; a girls' school incorporated with the adjacent church, which had managed to survive the bombings; and then, the arts centre itself ... all of these rise above a common podium level which contains formal crisscrossing stretches of broad rectangular waterways, bordered by public pedestrian spaces.

Lamont Road keeps a tight rein on the detailing consistencies of the project's 1950's British Brutalism; and as a result, the entire project one day will acquire such an iconic status as a pure example of this historical style, across the entire development, that in 2001, it will be granted Grade Two heritage listing – something sadly, that Joe Chamberlin will not live to see, passing away in 1978; just short of his sixtieth birthday. Joe, as the senior architect, is a formidable personality, driving the vision of the entire project to its conclusion. Prior to studying architecture, he had initially studied law; and this reflects in his abilities as a forceful debater, of almost lethal ability, on important issues and a strong driving political figure in the entire process. He is a master at handling people on all levels and during this time, I am privileged to observe his almost awesome abilities in this context. He stands as one of the grand old men of modern English architecture.

These two Lamont Road partners share a peculiar relationship with a third member of this team: Joe's wife, Jean, who acts as office manager and filing officer; and her personality is almost as formidable as Joe's. Her office and method of work are a marvel to behold: there is not one filing cabinet anywhere in evidence ... instead, the long, light-filled room which acts as her office has its side walls lined with soldierly stacks, shoulder to shoulder, of manilla folders containing individual files, all neatly standing up to somewhat around knee height. Running down the centre of the room, are two more such rows, carefully ranged back to back ... and the most amazing feat of all is that, at any single point in time, Jean knows exactly where an item and its file is!

These three – Joe, Jean and Christoph: the Barbican Trinity – live together in an unlikely menage a trois, in their house on their own little island in the Thames. There, Christoph (being the youngster of the cohabiting threesome) is treated almost as their child, as he bears the responsibilities of cooking, washing-up and taking out the garbage. Christoph is Swiss and characteristically, carries that finely-honed watch-precision banner proudly, with respect to coordinating the entire fine-detailing continuity of the Barbican project, from the ridged, hacked and hammered brutalist concrete surfaces and the way they relate to each other, down to the very type and placement of the least doorknob or light switch. He confesses to me once, as he stands over my shoulder while I work away at my drawing board, how much he had enjoyed draughting and how he misses it in his present role. He is a gentle, approachable man and has none of the overpowering presence of Joe. All these three are large people – not fat; just big people with big personalities and it is amusing sometimes in meetings, when Christoph is beginning to get too carried away with something of his own concern, to hear Joe boom out, as if to a child, 'Shut up, Christoph! Shut up!' This happens on quite a regular basis in meetings where the two of them are concerned. Joe is not the ogre he might seem however – he is simply the owner of a giant mind with an awesome background training. He always knows just where to draw the line and gently pull back. I have been present in meetings with the leader of my theatre team, John Connaughton, when Joe has been tearing strips off John over some matter or other, to the point where John is fast approaching a level of great humiliation; at this stage Joe will draw back, reach out a forgiving hand and pull John back up to the light, as a kindly father would, comfort and reassure him. Afterwards, the pair of us will leave to walk back up the Fulham Road to our own office as if nothing had ever transpired. Such is the respect which Joe commands.

* * * * *

WHEN I FIRST JOIN the office, I am assigned to the team headed by George Agabad, an Armenian architect looking after the Guildhall School of Music and Drama: the first component of the Arts Centre to be completed. There is to be a small greenhouse at podium level atop the Guildhall. This small greenhouse will be an extension of the half-acre conservatory which will eventually crown the adjacent theatre component. At this stage, these glass structures are in a conceptual state, requiring fine detailing of the glazed envelope and the steel structure which is destined to support it – this will be my initial responsibility on the theatre team. The structure consists of three-dimensional triangulated trusses, continuous in form from the podium up, through the glazed walls and across the glass roof slopes, to eventually come together at their apex against the upper regions of the double-height fly-tower of the theatre (the purpose of its existence is to soften and downplay the bulk of that large concrete digit arising from the podium to house this taller-than-usual fly-tower)... the entire structure to be fully-welded from round tubular-steel sections. I must satisfy the office with my handling of this small, trial-rendered extension from the later main conservatory. At its completion, I am to be moved across to form a part of the theatre team headed up by John Connaughton, an Irish architect with whom I shall form a close friendship for the remainder of my time in London; and for some time afterwards, until we sadly, eventually lose touch across the world's distance – and the distractions of other lives to be lived in other hemispheres.

So long before the genesis of the European Union, CPB is nothing short of containing its own league of nations. Lamont Road is populated by a staff of mainly Swiss, Indians and Pakistanis. Our own office here in Sydney Mews is the absolute multinational core of the practice. We have gentlemanly David Yeatman, soon to be followed when he takes early retirement, by John Honor, as office principals; Penny Hitchcock (later to be married to an Italian-Swiss architect, Andrea Cenci di Bello), as office manager; Sarah Fawcett, secretary-receptionist and little John-someone, architect; all of whom make up the main English contingent. In addition to these, we have myself, Phil Ward and Greg Runnegar – Australians, all from Brisbane, along with John Shephard from Adelaide; John Connaughton, Irish representative, as Theatre team leader; Ron, our resident Scott; Tony

Samson from South Africa; Girma Moges, from Ethiopia; Pierre Folliet, from France; Aart Verbeck, from Holland, heading up the Catering Block and Library team; Guillermo Gil, from Argentina; Pia, a pretty girl from Chile; Ashok Kumar, from India via Germany, married to a Swedish girl and with the two most-beautiful mocha-coloured children; a Swede, whose name now escapes me; Hans Ramsauer from Switzerland and Bernard Balmer from Bern in Switzerland, who will become a long-term friend for the next forty-five-plus years.

The Sydney Mews office is just a short walk down Sydney Place from South Kensington Tube Station, around the corner into the Fulham road and through the arch beside the pub, into the lane leading to our front door. The office is on two connected open levels; the mezzanine overlooking the ground floor around three sides of an open well, with a full height window rising up the forth side and over the central roof. It is light and airy, open and interconnected, friendly and warm ... and I will enjoy every moment of the next three years under its nurturing roof. These are all, most-interesting people. Whenever a personal telephone call is put through, one can expect to hear any one of about eight languages spoken ... even now, I can still hear Guillermo (William) Gill, as he will regularly and enthusiastically outburst to a friend's inaudible remark with, 'Aah! Fantastico! Fantastico!'

MY FATHER'S GHOST: A MEMOIR

Morton Court Hotel, now named 'The Nadler', Kensington.

82 Redcliffe Gardens, Kensington.

MY FATHER'S GHOST: A MEMOIR

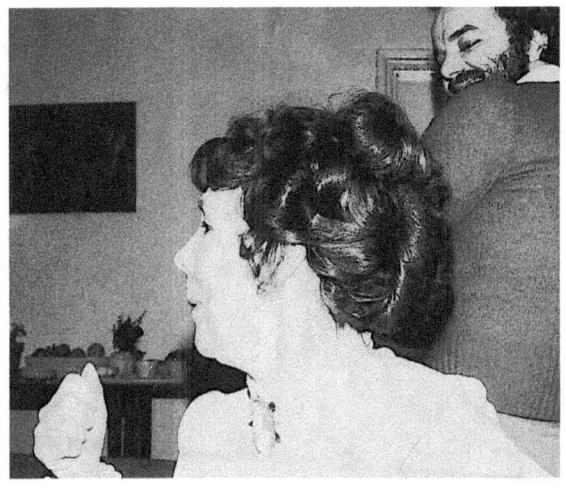

Mrs Moysey, our charming landlady at Redcliffe Gardens, 1974.

One Sunday afternoon in Hyde Park, London, the summer of 1974.

With Jane, Mrs A & Maurine in Hyde Park, late summer of 1974.

Sydney Mews today ... the entrance through the archway & so, our office.
Our local occupied ground & first floors to left of the arch.

10

A Flat of my Own at Last

SHORTLY AFTER JOINING Messrs Chamberlin, Powell and Bon, events at 82 Redcliffe Gardens take a turn for the better – Jane's mother, Mrs A, has kept her ear close to the ground for me and one evening, sends me downstairs to see our dear Mrs Moysey. These particular flats are not easily-occupied; in that they are only ever let on the basis of personal reference. Mrs Moysey is pleased with me and has three flats approaching changeover at the end of their current lease. One of them can be mine. I shall have to wait some weeks for this to happen but there it is: my accomodation needs are resolved.

    Back at the office, Tony Samson hears of my good news and offers his own flat during the interim. He and his wife, Bodge (Brigitte), along with their two boys, Guy and Dominic, are about to holiday in Southern Ireland for two weeks and, with the thought of saving me any further rent at Morton Court while acquiring themselves a caretaker while they are gone, offers me their flat in

Pimlico while I wait for my own glorious flat to become available. After work on the Friday before their weekend departure, we slip into our pub just outside the office for a game of darts over a pint or two of Guinness; as has become a regular office ritual. Then he takes me home, to meet Bodge, along with the boys, and to familiarise me with their flat, which I will move into with assistance from Maurine, after work on the Monday. As Bodge prepares dinner for us, he introduces me to a nip of poitin, the Irish moonshine, which takes my breath away completely for the next ten minutes, and then he says, 'Oh! You'd best meet Age while you are here this evening. He'll be in and out occasionally over the time while you're staying.'

Age Guinnessy is a young Irish architect, who had once also worked at CPB for a time ... that is, until one morning when the office cleaning lady came in a little earlier than usual, only to find washing strung on a line through the lower office, a long row of empty Guinness bottles adorning the high-set sill of our glazed wall to the lane and two bodies, still unconscious in their sleeping bags under the downstairs draughting tables – Age and his girlfriend, long-time squatters in the office. The cleaner involuntarily screams, faints, recovers and reports, whereupon Age is summarily-dismissed.

The flat in Pimlico occupies the upper-most two-and-one-half floors of the four storey house; and the top floor, which contains the boys' bedroom, is one long space within the slate-clad mansard roof. We ascend to this large room and Tony crosses over, opens one of the gable windows and steps out into the box gutter bordering the edge of the roof. I follow, not altogether confidently ... we stand with our knees beside a very-low parapet, while the mansard roof rises up to our right; and to our left, is the street, four stretched-out stories below, flanked by an iron-spiked picket fence. Tony shuffles along to the end where a ladder leads up to the exposed flattened top of the roof, to which we now ascend. There, above what feels to be the very top of the world in this insane moment, we shake hands with this mad Irishman who is building a twenty-foot canoe up there, as if it is the most natural thing in the world to do. The skeletal timber carcass reclines along the roof, resembling the remains of some large marine mammal lying amongst lengths of fresh lumber, surrounded by his tools. He's an easy, amiable fellow and we chat happily away up there in the late afternoon's light, then to descend again the way we came and to sit down to Bodge's excellent dinner. In the morning, they will depart for Ireland. The instructions are that if my new flat is still not ready when they return, then I am welcome to stay on until it is.

When Monday comes, Maurine helps me to move my luggage in after work and stays on for a light meal. I have told her about Age and we go upstairs to the attic room to check if he is again up there on the roof. What greets us when we open the door, is the timber carcass intact, lying diagonally across the now-rearranged boys' room, complete with his collection of timbers and tools ... but there is no sign of Age. He has somehow, over the weekend, with the family gone, (ingeniously or madly?) contrived to manoeuvre the beast over the edge of the roof and in through the dormer window to its present position, where he continues to work on it most evenings over the following fortnight. I hear him in the distance up there, hand-sawing and tap-tap-tap hammering away, until one Friday evening I go up to check on his progress ... and he is gone, along with the canoe, materials and tools – all vanished! Six months later, when Maurine has moved into her new flat, not far from Earl's Court Station and while I am visiting, I will stroll down her street to again discover Age with his canoe; still working away feverishly at it in the garage of another of his nearby friends – obviously a more convenient, safe and civilised environment in which to continue his project.

Tony and the family finally return and my promised flat is still occupied; so I stay on in Pimlico with them. They are all easy to live with and happy to have me there as a somewhat junior part of the family. They have an interesting collection of friends who drop in and out of their kitchen for enlightened evenings. Amongst these regular visitors is a likeable stained glass artist by the name of Roddy Friend, with whom I strike up an immediate friendship. Roddy is a recent graduate of the Royal College of Art: some few years older than myself, fascinating and very easy to relate to. Some of his post-graduate submissions at this time, involve no 'coloured' glass as such at all, being simply large clear-glass half-convex on one face only discs, flat on the other, which are silicone-cemented to large sheets of plate glass, on which they proceed to magnify portions of the world seen through them.

At the same time, he presents a rather esoteric character, with a tremendous interest in colour-healing: healing through the transmission of coloured light via his stained-glass creations. He belongs to a group of friends with similar philosophical interests: of mystic matters and of people whom I have never encountered before; consequently, we spend many evenings after the others at Pimlico have retired to bed, sitting in their kitchen as he tells me of these things – the likes of Madam Blavatsky and the theosophists; George Gurdjieff and his disciple, Ouspensky. This is all excitingly-new to me and in the times which follow, I purchase various copies of both Gurdjieff and Ouspensky, which continue to occupy a space in my library; and though eventually we will lose touch, I will not forget my brief friend, Roddy. I recently discover through Mr Google that he appears to be extant as I write this, living and producing stained glass, pastels and music from Andalucia in Spain.

There come occasional people who pass through our lives (sometimes, be it ever so briefly) who leave such marks in the sand, for whatever reason, that they never wash away ... Roddy was one of those. Distance and the years often place them beyond our reach but we continue to remember and wonder whatever became of them; how did they survive; or did they? I find there are many people beyond the ken, whom I wish I might still be able to converse with; to say, 'Do you remember when? So, how was your life? Are you happy?' Somehow, they remain important to me, even in their extended absence.

* * * *

MY FLAT AT 82 Redcliffe Gardens finally becomes available and I say goodbye to the Samsons and their household, which has happily nurtured me through these past four weeks at 125 Warwick Way, Pimlico. Eventually, there will be a big farewell party here for the Samsons themselves, before they move off to the next adventure of their lives, in Fiji; which I gather, for them is part of the nomadic way in which they follow their lives.

The flat I move into – my first very-own flat here – is charming; as are all of Mrs Moysey's flats at Number Eighty-two ... as is Mrs Moysey herself. Mine is on the first floor at the front, above the long street which forms Redcliffe Gardens. It is just a couple of doors removed from Redcliffe Square and, located on the first floor, has a large bay window overlooking the street. It is a large, roomy bedsitter with, one step down to the side, a kitchen with small built-in eating nook and a bathroom. It is fully-equiped right down to the last teaspoon and if one needs anything else, our dear landlady will have it there by the morrow. There is a laundry service which calls once a week: a cardboard suitcase comes with the flat, in which to leave all laundry for collection and return, in the ground floor lobby – and the cost is most-reasonable. Amongst its furnishings are some lovely antique pieces, including a magnificent, tall roll-top oak writing bureau with many compartments, including some concealed secret ones. There is some traffic noise on this side of the house and very little direct sunlight manages to make its way in ... but it is light and airy, and cosy.

We celebrate Jane's birthday here, when we all pitch in to buy her a real, silver Dunhill cigarette lighter – since she covets the one I have managed to buy for myself; from the very House of Dunhill in Jermyn Street. I cleverly conceal it within the deep pocket which I have laboriously cut into the body of a truly-boring and heavy, old hardcover medical register, purchased from a second-hand bookshop nearby ... initially she is disappointedly-nonplussed, then delighted as she discovers my ruse. She coaches me in playacting and in mime here, while she prepares me for my role in 'Johnson'. We have some very civilised dinners together here – Jane, Mrs A, Maurine and I ... and Billy comes down from Market Harborough to visit on occasions and bring me the very-latest but for myself fateful, updates on Kathy and Mary's progress ... and through the meantime, I continue to settle in and enjoy my life at what has now become my own enjoyable office.

* * * * *

And meanwhile, at CPB

HERE IN THE OFFICE, enduring friendships are being forged: John Connaughton in charge of my theatre team, Pierre and his wife Mary, Penny our clerical mainstay, 'Fantastico' Guillermo Gill and Switzer Bernard who helps me to brush up my almost-forgotten high-school German, while I help him to strengthen his faltering hold on English ... we sit at our desks, back to back in the office: something which aids our two-way tutoring. This will be a friendship which endures across two hemispheres and the rest of our lifetimes. The other friendships will endure for a time after I finally leave, to return home to Brisbane but over time, as must so often happen, distance and individual lives to be lived will reign supreme and tenuous threads will be slowly, or quickly, weakened and eventually broken. There is a kind of gentle sadness in this ... some parts of these lives will slip away one day, into a lost realm of final obscurity; threads will be lost and assume the qualities of a dream, of which one wonders, 'Was it ever lived – or simply, dreamt?' Oh, to be able to pick up the threads again and resume some conversations ....

John will eventually retire to live one day (wrapped in a vaguely-academic cloak, I should think ... he always had something of that quality to him), on a houseboat in Cambridge. His flat at Nottinghill Gate in this time, has all the air of an eccentric academic bachelor ... the centre of the main room holds a double-sided stand of tall industrial shelving which contains stack upon stack of neatly-folded used newspapers. He himself, has all of the characteristics of an old world academic, spending much of his leisure time in the Victoria and Albert Museum: which he insists, one could visit every day of a standard lifetime and still not see everything on display.

He came to London straight after his graduation from Trinity College in Dublin and has been in love with this metropolis ever since. We share many afterwork visits to our local, at the entry to Sydney Mews, during which, on one occasion, he hands on to me an observation he was given by a once-mentor of his, when he first arrived here ... 'London is a whore but she does insist on being treated like a lady.' – and that is it! He has, I suspect, a secret cache of very interesting friends, of which I see only the tip of the iceberg. On yet another afterwork occasion, I am introduced to his friend, Laurie Lee, who returns to meet with us again on the following week, bearing for me a signed, boxed set of his trilogy containing 'Cider With Rosie.' I, in my turn, have quickly come to share the same love for this grand old city, feeling more completely and naturally at home here than I will ever feel anywhere else. And, when I do eventually leave her, I shall carry a terrible homesickness with me which will never truly leave my side.

Pierre Folliet and his wife, Mary, will leave London before I do, moving back to Paris; and then, sometime after I myself have left London, they will move back to New York – in Mary's home country. Pierre and Mary are fantastic friends here in the interim – Pierre's family are from the countryside somewhere outside of Paris, where he earned his architecture degree; Mary is from Minnesota originally but gained her arts degree in New York. They were accidentally caught up in the students' Paris riots of 1968 ... not involved but, turning the corner into another street one day, suddenly found themselves terrifyingly in the midst of police, students, batons and tear gas. They have been so closely bound together for so long, that Mary has become as Parisian as Pierre has become New Yorker. Pierre is warmhearted, with a fine sense of humour and a balanced love for his profession. Mary is likewise, warmhearted but a fervent feminist and poet who will never forgive what she believes Ted Hughes did to Sylvia Plath, blaming him fully for her self-inflicted early demise. After Mary sees the bound copy of my poems to Kathy produced prior to Kathy's departure, she herself is inspired and we three, subsequently spend one wonderful summer of Saturday afternoons (where we have access to the book-binding facilities at the Lamont Road office), producing an edition of some 130 hardcover copies of Mary's poems, titled 'Modern Styles' – Pierre would provide the drawn illustrations (reproduced appropriately, on dyeline draughting film). I continue to carry about me, my own inscribed copy of this now-rare publication.

Every Saturday that summer, we spend our afternoon copying, trimming, gluing, clamping, linoprinting the board covers, trimming again and attaching them to the text ... until finally, we are done. Each such evening we return to their flat in Finborough Road (not very far from my own in Redcliffe Gardens), where Pierre, now as the French chef, prepares delicious meals for us while we listen to mostly-jazz (it is during one of these times that I discover the wonderful Betty Carter, as they play the only album she has ever produced at this point –with Ray Charles). I stay over and in the mornings, the French chef performs his magic over again with omelette breakfasts. Their bedroom overlooks the old and very-picturesque Brompton Cemetery, full of trees and songbirds and there, on one memorable night at the end of our book production, we three celebrate and sit the night away, emptying a new bottle of Armagnac while Mary reads her poems to us until the bottle is spent, dawn is gently lighting-up the trees and stone slabs, while the birds send up their first twitterings of the day.

I have already discovered in myself, a closet Francophile and when I express a desire to master more French, Mary declares, 'Oh, my dear, if you want to learn French properly, then you must have a French lover' ... and proceeds, if obliquely, to do just that in arranging for my taking lessons in the language with her good friend, Sylvie, who works at and lives in a flat housed in the premises of, Alliance Francaise de Londres, conveniently close by on the Cromwell Road at that time. In a short while, we do in fact, find ourselves more than simply friends and Mary is ever-so-pleased for us. Unfortunately, Sylvie's English remains much better than my French will ever be and, with our blossoming involvement in each other taking charge, my progress in the language falls behind. Mary is well-pleased with her own publication and enjoys good sales amongst her friends and close associates. In New York many years later, Mary will find her niche as a literary consultant and editor; meantime, Pierre will continue to practice architecture there, whilst also describing himself as a painter and poet.

Penny Cenci di Bello will continue to live in London with her architect husband, Andrea and their son, Lorenzo, where they will one day, amongst their other achievements, become noted for their restoration of their home during the 1990s at No.41-42 Cloth Fair, reputed to be the oldest surviving house in London. Penny will also rise to occupy a much-respected-by-her-peers position as a local councillor for the City of London's Ward of Farringdon, while Andrea will continue operating as an independent architectural consultant.

During my years, we forge a comfortable work-friends friendship with each other. Andrea works as an architect in another office in these times. His mother is a noted Italian-Swiss ceramics artist who once exhibited with Picasso. I eventually will meet her, a sweet diminutive woman with very little English, when she comes to London and I share Christmas lunch with them in my final year here. He and his mother share strong connections with Florence ... it is told that only boy-children of the royal household of Florence may be baptised in the baptistry of the Duomo there and at this date, Andrea is said to be the last to have been granted that privilege.

Penny and Andrea love trawling the weekend markets and eventually, they amass so much loot from their forays that they must attempt to effect some serious culling. They acquire a weekend stall to unload some of their excess, in the antiques section of Portobello Road, up in Notting Hill; and it performs so well for them on their first weekend, that it becomes a second occupation for them ... Penny mans, or womans, the stall each Saturday while Andrea scours the cheaper stalls at the bottom of the hill, buying select items to up-price and resell from their store at the top. They turn quite a tidy profit from this exercise, whilst continuing to involve themselves in the very things which had enhanced their weekends previously. We regularly share mostly-Chinese meals in back of Soho and on occasions, home-cooked meals at their own flat, where Andrea is the star chef ... he buries himself behind the glass door, alone in their kitchen, wearing his high toque blanche, the white traditional chef's hat, swathed in vast billows of steam, at the far end of their hallway, while the rest of us sit it out in their lounge; here, their smart Burmese cat (who also accompanies Penny to the office), cleverly entertains us by displaying her door-latch-opening skills.

During my penultimate year in London, P&O conduct a promotion for their cross-Channel ferry service as part of which deal, for the price of a standard one-day ticket, every passenger receives a carton of Rothmans cigarettes and bottle of red label Johnny Walker on the return trip – gratis! We take up the offer, of course. There are the four of us, including one other of their friends. We all sleep over at their flat and rise at 4.00am to be down in Dover in time at 7.00am, to catch the first ferry to Boulogne-sur-Mer on the Channel coast of France. Once there, we spend a wonderful fifteen hours, mostly-engaged in following Andrea the Chef, as he feverishly leads us from one supermarket to another, excitedly sourcing products and ingredients for his kitchen, which are impossible to find in London. Our pay-offs for our docile accompanying on this gastronomic odyssey, are that we get to have whistle-stops all over town to snack at coffee shops, patisseries and bars along the way. I am astounded when he pays five pounds to purchase one black truffle contained inside the tiniest little can ... we do get to enjoy the shared product of this recklessness later, at Christmas time; when as part of our feast, he prepares a ballotine de canard, created from a fully-boned, minced whole duck, embellished and manipulated back into its original, kept-intact skin – and bearing our truffle, finely distributed throughout the contents. This forms the centrepiece of our lunch that Christmas; and follows my introduction to, for me, a new vegetable experience in our simple but appetising entree of steamed artichoke with a vinaigrette.

This is the meal that Andrea's ceramicist mother attends, sits by me and instructs me in the method of attacking this delicious thistle.

When I last saw him, Guillermo was seeking to follow the path of the artist-painter cum architect. From the little I can glean all this time later, he did continue on as an architect in London but I can find no recorded evidence of any great success for him in the art field. At the time, whilst we were still working in the office together, he had moved into a large flat with one very big living room to use as a studio of sorts; in Pitt Street, just around the corner from my own flat when I later lived in Gordon Place. While still performing his architect role at CPB, Guillermo has decided to change his persona after dark, to that of the intense Latin artist.

In his new flat, he spends his evenings locked away in front of enormous, long, floodlit canvasses, painting what are more like murals in their scale. He works in acrylic and draws his sources from Argentinian newspapers and magazines, while he creates vast assemblages of people from society's pages; they crowd together, slightly larger than life, in gently-muted subtle tones and carry about them, something of the boldly-stylised, rounded lumpy manner of the great Mexican muralists like Diego Rivera and Siqueiros. He photographs these mammoth works and sends them off to journalistic sources in Argentina where, I believe, they are published ... he is seeking his own exhibition there. I don't know whether this ever happens but one thing is sure: that he does continue his architectural existence in London where, I understand, he does acquire his coveted residency status, which many emigres sought to gain in those years.

Barmy Bernard Balmer from Berne (his own self-joke) will move back to his parents home on the outskirts of Berne, where I will visit before my own UK stay runs its final course. There, he will at last find the true love he seeks, in the form of his best friend's sister, Ruth; whom he will marry and with whom, father one child: a daughter, Annabel. All of that is another story, best-saved for a later time.

When we cement our friendship at the Barbican's office, he is involved with a pretty, young Persian woman, Annahita. Her parents are wealthy industrialists back in Tehran and with the rise of the Ayatollah Khomeini and the numbered days for the Shah, they have sent Annahita Sallapush to London and safety. Here, she enrols at the Sir John Cass College of Art, studying printmaking (In the current time, it is referred to simply as The Cass or the Aldgate Bauhaus, having transformed into its present form in 2012). The three of us share many meals together in Soho; mostly Chinese and Greek ... one evening, in our favourite subterranean Greek cellar, she tells us of her studies at Cass and I mention a very-fleeting past moment concerning a screen printing request from a friend – on which I had never followed through. Annahita is a most-impetuous young woman and, when we all gather for a meal the following week, she informs me that she has in fact enrolled me in the printmaking course at John Cass.

By this time, I have consigned myself to a passive role in any theatrical future undertaking; and so, I think, 'Why not?' ... so, along I go – and I am hooked. From that point on, printmaking at Sir John Cass becomes my life away from the office. It starts with one evening per week, which grows to two, then three evenings and eventually, Saturday afternoons also. It does become a magnificent obsession.

Aart Verbeck never really becomes a friend as such; of anyone in the office so far as I can tell; his is more a matter of treating with mutual respect, from a safe distance. Aart is of a similar age, blusteringly confident and consumed by ambition. He is tall and athletically-robust, handsome in a Dutch sort of way, with his blue eyes, thick and healthy blond hair accompanying his Frans Hals luxuriant, blond handlebar moustache and clipped, well-formed speech ... a perfect Aryan specimen. He drives a green early model SAAB and has a lot to live up to. His father is a very-successful Dutch banker, his elder brother is likewise doing very-well in the European world of finance and Aart himself, has married a daughter of the Philips manufacturing family. His bar has been set very high ... and he chose to be an architect? Noble a profession as architecture might be (not just a profession but one of the creative arts), to the average practitioner it is not exactly a field in which to forge one's fortune; short perhaps of being the principal of a large successful firm.

It is obvious that this is the course which he believes he must pursue: to achieve a position as an associate or even junior partner in this firm. As a result, his bombastic nature, along with his naked ambition and sometimes ruthlessness, do not make the path to office friendships an easy one; even though he is not a bad person as such and probably hides a good heart somewhere ... no matter, his single-mindedness subjugates all other considerations in chasing his destiny. He has, at this point, managed to gain the role of senior architect for the Art Gallery, Library and Catering Block components of the project.

The ground and upper mezzanine levels of our office are connected by a single open stair, partly concealed from most of the office behind a supporting side wall. One afternoon, there issues a mighty crash, followed by a solid Thump, Thump, Thump! Responses cry out from the lower floor ...

Phil Ward: 'Shit! What was that?'

John Shephard: 'Aart just fell down the stairs.'

Little John (from the far corner, in his thin reedy voice, carrying just a hint of hopefulness): 'Is he dead?'

Aart has in fact, missed the edge of the tread, ascending the stair, from whence he bounced his large frame back to the bottom. He finally reappears at the top of the stair, red-faced and sheepish, his pride injured not so much by the responses, than by the clumsiness of the act itself. He eventually realises sometime future, that he will not attain greatness or fortune in this office and moves on. I believe he finally carves out a comfortable niche for himself in a large development company.

* * * * *

Printmaking at Sir John Cass

I AM SHOWING a ready aptitude for what I do here at John Cass and quickly gain a reputation for being the cleanest and tidiest printmaker in the studio. Richard is in charge of the screen-printing class, while David Brown looks after the etching group. When new screen-printers join the class, Richard sends them to me ... where, when the pulled prints hang down, row upon row to dry from the overhead rack, mine are the only ones which don't have a rash of coloured fingerprints adorning their exposed margins. I'm not overly-fussy – I'm simply ordered and methodical, as any self-respecting architect should be. I enjoy the founding of some good friendships with some very-talented artists: the likes of Bonnie Webb, a sweet girl from the north of England, who labours forever over the most finely-detailed, softly-coloured avenue of trees which I help her to name 'Sunset Boulevard', a copy of which still graces my walls; and Mirella Aprahamian, a Lebanese-Armenian mother of enormous creative talent and drive, who leaves me a number of mementos over the years, in her always-bright and colourful, highly-detailed screen-prints, of a never-ending creativity.

She and I often share a Tube ride together for part of our ways home after class; always stopping by at Blooms restaurant near the art school in Whitechapel, where we order corned beef on rye, freshly cut from the large, hot and incredibly-juicy slab which perpetually adorns a large board, in pride of place on their front counter. These famous sandwiches, in their plain brown paper bags, form a late dinner for us as we ride our train journey away from class. She and her family will eventually move to Canada, where she will go from strength to strength with her colourful art prints and vibrant originality. We manage to correspond for some time afterwards but eventually, as she moves her little family to Canada, time and distance wear many threads thin, and sadly, they become broken.

David Brown and his printmaker co-artist and friend, Ken Oliver, have a magnificent studio space in the East End, which I visit on occasion. The approach in the docklands area, is down a series of laneways between disused, tall old brick warehouse buildings; various characters lounge around the area, warming themselves around smoking fires issuing from empty old 44gallon drums ... a somewhat seedy approach. At E.Warehouse, there comes an unimposing set of raw concrete stairs, up four tall floors to a large, heavy, rust-encrusted single door ... which swings open to reveal a vast, wonderful studio space, high and light-filled, expansive, with large, heavy flatbed etching presses and drying racks, storage shelves – light and space, inspiring. On the far side, large, double, heavy-timbered bi-parting sliding high doors with their original lifting gantry beams projecting outwards, open to the Thames waterway, directly running by, a dizzying distance below. This is an Eden for artist-printmakers and Dave, with his friend, are so fortunate to have this stake in it.

There is one other member of our studio, not easily-forgotten ... I have no idea what her name is (we all knew her first name at the time but she kept pretty-much to herself and so, was quickly forgotten). She is an older woman and also a smoker, (as many of us are at this time in history) ... she is also the messiest printmaker this studio has ever seen. She mixes up far too much ink for her screen; it is far too thin; and she pours far too much of it into the well of her screen, for the squeegee to effectively transfer it cleanly through her screen stencils. The results are prints with ink deposited clumsily, overflowing far beyond where it should sit in the finished image. She is for us, fearsomely-older, with a well-fitting obstinance which refuses any form of advice or instruction; but the truly scary part arrives when it comes time to clean up our equipment ... there she stands, with very little of her excess of ink removed from the well of its frame, in which it continues to swim, aided by the half-bottle of mineral turpentine (which we all use for our final cleanup), as she proceeds to swab the whole sloshing mess of ink and turps, around and over the edges of the frame, using old rags and newsprint, while she leans over it and works away at this Herculean task ... with her glowing cigarette dangling from her slackened lips! Needless to say, on nights' endings such as these, the rest of us clean up very quickly and flee the studio, before she herself sets-in to housekeeping, with her boundless potential for violent self-immolation.

* * * * *

Meanwhile ...

BUT TO HEARKEN BACK to the main story, (you will get used to my wandering off like this. I have a poet friend these days who does this regularly, like Alice's White Rabbit – my friend has more rabbit holes than I will ever fall down) ... back at Redcliffe Gardens, we are moving towards the end of the year. The theatre at Ealing liked Jane's earlier shop window, with Ableman's 'Johnson', and she has now been given her first opportunity to mount a full play at Questors. The play she has chosen is a strange piece by the Spanish playwright, Fernando Arrabal, named 'The Architect and the Emperor of Assyria'. It is a two-man psychological encounter in an isolated setting (presumably on a desert island, but it could just as easily take place within the sharing of a prison cell), where the 'Emperor' relates and acts out his fantasies to his 'Architect', as both audience and co-playmate. David Girling (the doctor from our 'Johnson' piece) plays the role of the emperor, against that of Michael Moriarty, as the hapless architect. My role is to design and build the set on an absolute shoestring budget (the theatre arrangement we use, is reminiscent of that which Doug Anders and I used for 'Electra', with a three-quarter-round audience arrangement), take care of the graphics design for the posters, and to produce a series of masks, which the players intermittently select from a large chest onstage and briefly wear, as they adopt personalities from the emperor's past life.

There are six masks in all, which represent various family members and friends of the emperor. I spend my evenings at home for the next month or more, sitting with a large coil of pliable wire, pliers and soldering equipment, as I create the bare-bones-and-sinews framework masks; through which the players themselves might be seen, as they don them after the manner of fencing masks, which will leave their hands free to perform after adopting them. The end results are terribly-successful and, after the show is over and done, everyone involved keeps one of the masks as a memento; one of these continues to grace my studio walls even now.

The time is now mid-November and the days have shortened; as have dropped the temperatures. There comes one evening, towards the end of this mask fabrication in the ending of my office day, when I finally put aside my soldering iron and retire to soak in a hot bath before bed. It is around 11.00pm and chilly. I need two unwind. So, I run a very-full hot soak in my sarcophagus-sized cast iron bath. Stretched out in it with my toes extended, I can only just touch the far end of the bath while still keeping my head above water. I have my current novel in hand, lower myself in and begin reading ... before I know it, I awake, to find the book lying on the floor beside my bath and the time is just 3.00am; the bath water is stone cold, but not so cold as the frigid air outside the bath when I seek to arise. I could have drowned! But no ... I dry myself and scuttle off to bed, for a now-abbreviated sleep before setting off for a new-day at the office.

As this year's end and Christmas approaches, I am assigned the task at the office, of coming up with some original decorations for the season. We have a wonderful large void in the space between our upper mezzanine level and the ground floor, with the towering glazed wall which rises up the fourth side of the space and back over it at roof level. Looking back at it now, I realise that what I manage to produce is a Joan Miro-meets-Alexander Calder-type giant mobile filling that vast space ... discs and hoops and crescents formed from basket-weaving cane with coloured tissue paper and mirror foil stretched across them – all suspended by nylon fishing line from criss-crossing wooden dowels, hanging and swinging from each other, carefully balanced in our two-storey void. It is enthusiastically-received and forms a colourful centrepiece to the office for many weeks to come.

In the meantime, I have moved flat – to the one I had originally been assigned, one floor up and at the rear of the house. Cosy and intimate as the first flat had been, it was a little street-noisy and admitted little sunlight but this new flat is light and bright, overlooks the pretty gardens backing this house and a large number of its neighbours; and is quiet and sunny ... filled with light and winter warmth, the kitchen is new and the bathroom generous. It is here that

I make the masks for the Arrabal, come short of drowning in a midnight bath and enjoy some tender and intimate moments with Maurine. It is a beautiful flat. The Sunday luncheons with the effervescent Mrs Moysey continue and Jane, with her mother, the adorable Mrs A, continue to live directly above me, on the next floor; Jane's good friend, the talented and diminutive actor, Neil, freshly-arrived from Brisbane, moves in with me for a time, until our difference in lifestyles and sexual preferences make it impossible to do so any longer. At this point, I am sadly brought to realise that I cannot continue to afford to live here alone and on my own resources any longer without risking insolvency. Painful as it is, I will have to surrender this little haven and find myself another home. Mrs Moysey is good about it but there is nothing either of us can realistically do. Maurine has by now, found her own share accomodation, away from the Atkins and further up the road, on the other side of Earl's Court Station some little bit and I myself, begin looking anew for a home.

MY FATHER'S GHOST: A MEMOIR

82 Redcliffe Gardens: My first flat above the street, cosy but noisy, 1974.

Jane receives her Dunhill lighter, a birthday present from all of us.
Dinner party in the first flat, with her Mum Mrs A, Maurine & I, 1974.

My second flat, 82 Redcliffe Gardens, one floor up, above the rear garden, 1974.

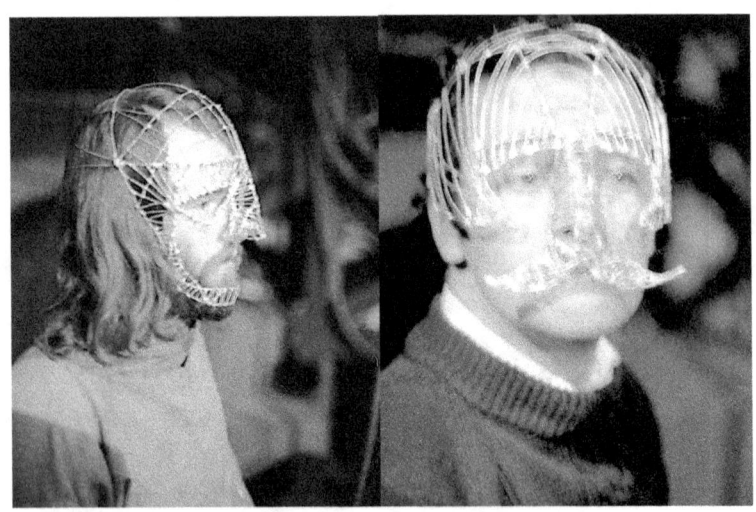

Richard & David wearing two of my masks for our production at Questors: Arrabal's 'The Architect and The Emperor of Assyria', Ealing 1974.

11

Gordon Place: A New Home

I ENDEAVOUR not to move very far from where I currently live, and chase up potential bed-sitters in the Kensington-Knightsbridge area, so as not to be too far from my friends or the office. Initially it is discouraging – some of them are truly less than civilised, being little more than a room with all other facilities shared – all other! ... one of them, which boasts a shared eat-in kitchen, actually has the cast-iron shared bath, also sitting right in the middle of the kitchen! I am not greatly-heartened.

Then I find Number 20, Gordon Place, Kensington ... a modest bed-sit, compact, but a suitable, neat haven in many ways. It is a short walk in behind the junction of Kensington High Street and

Kensington Church Street; Kensington Church Walk, with its hairdresser and other specialty shops, makes for a pleasant alternative connection down to the High Street; all this is close to the High Street tube station and one can bus, tube or walk to the office at South Kensington; up the hill, to the top of Church Street, lies Nottinghill Gate and Portobello Road markets; eastwards across Church Street, lies Kensington Palace, Kensington Gardens and Hyde Park. In the same vicinity, immediately south of the Gardens and Park, lie the Science Museum and the ever-wonderful Victoria and Albert Museum: a facility which John Connaughton maintains one could visit every day of one's life and still never see everything contained behind its walls.

My new bed-sit lodges to one side and one floor above the street entry at Number Twenty, with a lovely big bay window overlooking same; it contains one large, high-ceilinged room with a sizeable wardrobe built-in, corner kitchenette behind a door-height screen wall and a smallish but very effective built-in gas fireplace. The toilet, house telephone and two bathrooms are off the landing outside, shared with the one other flat on this floor, which is occupied by a genteel spinster; the ground floor is of a similar arrangement; above us, is another like floor; and finally, a studio apartment sits within the mansard roof space above – this is occupied by a longterm tenant: the accomplished actor, William Squire, whom I sometimes meet and chat with, as we pass on the stairs. Bill Squire grew up in the same village as Richard Burton and took over from him in his role for 'Camelot' on Broadway. He is one of those sublimely-competent actors of stage, screen and television who never seems to be far from regular good work in his chosen field. In later years, he will voice the role of Gandalf in 'The Lord Of the Rings' annimation. He is most affable and a makes a good neighbour. When he informs me that he has taken the role of Polonius in Tom Stoppard's 'Rosencrantz and Guildenstern are Dead' in the

West End, I naturally, go to see the show. I already know it and have greatly enjoyed this play through a reading of it and it now pleases me to see my own neighbour from upstairs performing in this production.

Small and modest as it is, I enjoy my quiet and secluded life in this flat for the next two-plus years. This is now my home and I feel so very much in place here – I belong. Aside from Bill in the roof-space studio upstairs, every other resident appears to be one kind of middle-aged spinster or another: all are retiring, charming and friendly. Here it is that Guillermo Gil moves-in, practically around the corner, to inspire me in my own painterly endeavours; here, I eventually fall irreparably in love with Sooz who will haunt me (mostly in absentia) for another thirty years, as our paths briefly cross and collide, uncross and disentangle – never to actually be the One Grail, as I once imagined her to be; here, during one Christmas break, I read the entire 'Lord of The Rings' trilogy over ten cosily-cosseted-in-my-flat days (which master-work, all of my own work colleagues are currently reading, for themselves or to their own children ... or more likely, both); here, I embark on a tender but abbreviated relationship with my sweet French Sylvie, who will on occasion, occupy a place of sometimes, gentle regret in the background of my life; here, I will for a very brief moment, encounter a delightful face from the past in Bridie, and be taken unawares one evening by Bernard's once girlfriend, Annahita in a moment of weakness; and here finally, where I shall enter a relationship with Carmel, bridging the final path back to my family in Brisbane. Small as it is, this flat nurtures me happily through the most formative years of my life here. The sense of nostalgia it evokes even now, forty-plus years later, is overpowering ... it is for a moment, home.

From my bay window, I look across to the steeple of St Mary Abbots Church, at the bottom of Church Walk; below me, at the corner of my street, is the Elephant and Castle pub and just around the corner from that, are the London Art Bookshop and Academy Bookshop, the Equinox Bookstore: holding an enormously-varied esoteric and related, content; and Cassidy's, the best hamburger shop ever: which venue, often provides my dinner as I arrive home from a late printmaking class at John Cass – quality open burgers with chips and a glass of red wine, sometimes in the company of the late-evening waitress, sitting out on the footpath through the last of the quiet dusk, with gentle jazz playing discretely in the background ... before paying up and heading, just a matter of doors up, to my own quiet retreat.

My tiny kitchenette holds a few cupboards, a single sink and a very small stove with oven – but no refrigerator. The tiny stove and the comforting, inbuilt gas heater, glowing like a small stack of combusting bones in the recessed fireplace with mantlepiece overhead, are fed by a coin slot meter. My three sided bay window has very-deep reveals and sills; and this bay, on the side away from the morning sun's path, provides my refrigerator. Winter and summer, I keep my butter and milk out there on it, sitting in a wide, water-filled dish with a wet tea towel draped over it. When the remaining milk eventually turns, I strain the curds tight in a clean linen handkerchief, which I then hang and thus, turn them into cheese.

During my long, late and lazy Christmas mornings, when there is no office to attend and when most of my friends are out of London for the holiday break, I make a small batch of Soozie's own scone recipe in my tiny oven, to accompany fresh expresso from my tiny Bialetti (which I regularly forget to actually put water into while I am distracted by my own painterly efforts; after this, I must front up to the supplier's shop somewhere in the back of Soho, in order to once again replace the device's burnt-out rubber gasket) ... collect my current reading material, and head back to bed. The gas fire is a small but incredibly-efficient, pretty honeycomb of porcelain bones which glow a bright, friendly orange in the gentle gas flames during the cold weathers.

A cleaner (in actuality, the live-in landlady, a pleasant motherly matron on the ground floor and basement levels) comes in weekly, to tidy the flat and keep things looking spotless. Life here, whilst contained in an attractive but particularly-compact package, is comfortable, quiet and protective. In every direction through the streets surrounding me, exist abundant, always-interesting vignettes of inner-London life and its vast, ever-present variety. With the great convenience of my location, residing as I am here, close-in beside this city's great beating heart; and with such a convenient placement, regarding the proximity to my own place of very-happy and gainful employment, where could one live in London to enjoy any more of her comfortable distractions and richness than this tiny oasis in the heart of Kensington?

* * * * *

SO MUCH TRANSPIRES in this modest oasis over the course of my couple of happy years living here ... mostly small things but significant, memorable.

The dominant population of motherly matrons often invite me as I pass their doors, to come in for a cup of tea, a sherry, a scotch even. This never happens. I am always rushing out or coming home, looking forward to the sanctity of my own small nest; I am always apologising and reassuring with a 'Next time, perhaps'. One day, I am a little early and say, 'Well, just for a moment,' to the offer of a cup of tea from the ground floor resident as I come in. I explain that I am expecting Sylvie shortly and ask if we can leave the door ajar, so I can see when she arrives. We chat for longer than I intended and finally, I excuse myself and continue upstairs; only to find that Sylvie has in fact been and gone, leaving a small, cramped terse note attached to my door. Finding me not at home, she has climbed out of the landing window, across and onto the ledge of my left-open bay window (the one which doubles as my refrigerator), left items for our evening meal with Bernard and Annahita, and returned home to change ... this little journey takes place a considerable height above the street entry below.

SYLVIE

At least it's a luck
you don't close your windows
it's not more than two hours
I would have had to wait
behind a door.
I go home and come back
with your salad
at around eight!

These are happy times with Sylvie. I probably spend as much time living at her Alliance Francaise address as I spend in my own haven during this time. We have a jolly group of young French friends gather with us around Sylvie's kitchen table on Monday evenings. Jean Claude always goes home to his parents in the French countryside for the weekend; Mondays, he returns to us with the boot of his Volkswagon Beetle bursting with French Foodie items and we spend the evening devouring many of them over warm conversation. My comprehension of the language remains at a basic level but I understand enough to know that the subject matters are mostly of food and wine. On weekends, we wander the many Saturday markets like Petticoat Lane and Brick Lane, where so many weekend characters abound: outrageous spruikers and barkers, such as one with two ferrets running around inside his shirt, occasionally poking a head through between buttons to sniff the air, as he peddles his perfumes in Brick Lane; quiet, low-key older characters placed inert beside their estate jewellery tables, as ruminating figures from a past era ... a complete contrast to the trails up and down Portobello Road back in my own local area, where there are as many permanent shops to be found as there are weekend stalls.

During these times, the greater population of the office at CPB, besides taking on the lasting love affair with J.R.R. Tolkien which they pass onto their own children, they also exchange with each other, a passion for science fiction and specialised comic books. We share the sci-fi authors of this time and just uphill from my flat, towards Nottinghill Gate and off in a small lane to one side of Church Street, lies probably the best comic book shop of this era, at the Book and Comic Exchange; here, I discover a series of French hardcover comic books by Philippe Druillett, relating the adventures of a certain intergalactic hero by the name of 'Lone Sloane', simply amazing for their elaborate futuristic draughtsmanship, artwork and colour; which I am of course, compelled to acquire and keep for all time.

There eventually comes one Christmas season, when the ageing matron who shares my own floor disappears from public view for a number of days; at which time, having received no response to her door-knocks, our housekeeper-landlady lets herself into the flat to find her tenant prone on the floor with a broken hip ... amidst a sea of empty scotch bottles. It seems her doctor has recommended a small scotch before bed to assist sleep; only problem being that she is at the age where forgetfulness takes occasional residence and so, having forgotten the first drink, she has another – before bed, you understand. Well, one forgotten drink builds on another until, stepping on an empty bottle rolling around the floor, she goes down for the count. She will live but not unassisted. It is discovered that she has a sister, with whom she has not spoken, through some early conflict, for the past twenty years. With some difficulty, the sister is finally located and reunited with her; to share in her ongoing care, where the story has a sad but happy ending, of sorts. I, for my part, share a little gentle regret that I never stopped in to share that Scotch which she often offered me as I passed on the stairs to my bedsit ... or was there an element of guilt, given that there was obviously a touch of loneliness on her part?

Just around the corner from my flat, at number 51 Kensington Church Street where the street takes its first little uphill bend, is a delightful and popular little restaurant known as The Twin Brothers: popular, because the decor, the staff and owners are attractive and a little flamboyantly-theatrical as well as the food being excellent and economical (in these times, there is an abundance of good quality, cheap eateries from an eclectic choice of ethnic origins throughout London) ... I particularly remember a dish of Bismarck pickled herrings with sour cream, apples and walnuts. A review of the times from the 1976 publication 'Cheap Eats in London' read ...

"The Twin Brothers Restaurant is recognizable from the outside by a little striped awning and red fringed lamps in the windows. It is situated in Kensington Church Street, just where the road has a kink in it. Inside, there are more fringed lamps on gilded brackets, dark green and gold wallpaper, Murillo-like portraits and still lifes of fruit. Spindly wrought-iron chairs and gilt-framed mirrors give the place an air of a Viennese café, for this restaurant is owned and run by Helge and Detlef Schmidt, who are from Berlin and are, as the name of the restaurant implies, twin brothers. Helge, a blond giant who would look well as Siegfried, does the waiting; Detlef, who remains unseen, but who is presumably also a blond giant, does the cooking..."

The restaurant remains but in the current time, it, like my first lodgings, has undergone a change of ownership, decor and culinary style, now being known as 'Ffiona's' restaurant, specialising in home-grown British cooking.

Meanwhile, down from Church Street, on the High Street, lie the grand, seven-storey department stores of 'Barkers' along with the oh-so-chic and trendy, Art Deco-themed 'Biba's'.

'Biba's' is a London icon of the 1960s and 70s, once visited, never forgotten. Its marketing has a wonderful consistency, with its simple 1930s Deco graphics, where every floor is cleverly mood-lit and holding a single product range spread across its lofty vastness: homewares, men's, women's, children's, foodstuffs, all assembled with the air of a spacious, spotlighted marketplace. Every piece of packaging and wrapping carries somewhere, the unmistakeable Art Deco graphic motif of the Biba brand. The rooftop houses a glazed conservatory of a teahouse cafe set in a vast 6,000 square metre garden which spreads to the very edges of the enormous building and holds a strutting flamboyance of four pink flamingos, as its crowning glory.

Also in High Street, a couple of doors from Church Street, there lies a large antique hypermarket, where I am infected with my first glimpse of a Japanese netsuke. The entry from the High Street is recessed between a pair of large glass showcases. The right-hand case holds nothing but tier upon tier of Victorian porcelain-faced dolls ... staring, just staring at the viewer: the effect is just a little chilling. There is a single double-sided lane of stalls which loops from the entry down one side of the building, turning at the end, to return up the other side. There, at the turning point, is a stall holding amongst other objects, a small carving: an ivory and ebony figurine of a Japanese Noh Theatre character. It is exquisite – it squats in a typical pose, long-mane bewigged and flowing-robed, with a face which rotates to reveal comic/tragic features front and back ... what is called a trick netsuke. It is 'only' £27: a sum which I just cannot afford to commit myself to spend in these times of limited income. It remains in my consciousness for the next ten years until I discover my first such carving; this time it is affordable – back in another antique hypermarket, in my hometown of Brisbane.

A short distance to the east, lies the palace, Kensington Gardens, Hyde Park and Albert Hall. Slightly south-east, in an easy walking distance, lies the Victoria and Albert museum where, as John Connaughton certifies, one could spend a lifetime and still never see everything. A similar distance westwards from this hub that I occupy, lies the delightful Holland Park: a little piece of Beatrix Potter, where on a summers evening, we attend open-air theatre performances, reclining on comfortable deckchairs, armed with a glass of wine from the outdoor bar.

This is the 1970s and the years of power cuts due to the miners' strikes of this decade and often, the continuing threats of random bombings by the IRA to the inner London areas. It presents an ever present danger to which one becomes accustomed and ultimately, a little blasé. There is a Saturday afternoon when Maurine and I are casually wandering the upper reaches of Barker's Store in Kensington High Street; nothing specific, just window shopping. There are no lifts – just grand, broad flights of comfortable stairs between floors. We decide it is time to move on and begin our descent; for the first time, becoming conscious of how deserted the store seems to have suddenly become and how, one or two floors down, there appears a police presence: Bobbies urging us to quickly leave the store. As we reach the ground floor and exit into High Street, we find that what appears to be the entire population of the store, staff and customers alike, are ranged expectantly on the opposite side of the road, awaiting the explosion or 'all-clear', whichever eventuates. Of course, it is just one more false alarm.

During these times, it becomes a quite common occurrence (always at roughly 7.00am, while I breakfast and prepare for the office) that there will be heard a muffled but resounding 'Whoomph!' from somewhere further up the hill above my home. There are quite a number of embassy residences in the immediate area, with street parking only, available. When I arrive at my South Kensington office, some little time later, I learn that yet another embassy car has been targeted that morning. It is an everyday part of life which one calmly accepts and thinks nothing more of and where no one ever seems to actually be hurt by these incidents ... just expensive vehicles.

One summer's evening, I approach home in the twilight, after my John Cass printmaking class and, at the bottom of Gordon Place, an ageing bag- lady accosts me to ask the time of day. There ensues an extended conversation, friendly and not at all unpleasant, in the course of which, she informs me that she had served, as a nurse, under 'Monty' (Field Marshal Montgomery) during WW2. She is at this time, on her way to her evening employment serving at a soup kitchen in Soho, where she is operating as an undercover agent, collecting information in an effort to break a major drug ring. This could be fanciful; or it could be true – she comes across very convincingly. All I know is that, some weeks later, the newspapers do carry headlines of a major drug-bust in the area, which had been in operation for some months and has now succeeded.

* * * * *

IN RETROSPECT, I realise that I was more impacted by the circumstances of my young marriage's collapse than I gave it credit in those times. I drift between several women during my residence in this London W8 flat; each of whom, I imagine, is the answer to my dreams: the grail which I steadfastly seek ... and it seems, may never find. I must admit to a lifetime of being a hopeless (or is it helpless?) romantic – a state which suggests itself as being more and more delusional in this current twenty-first century. I am not deterred. I begin once more to write poetry up there in my own little garret, just above my quiet street ... now, I trust, with a new awareness for its form and craftsmanship; and of the Oriental forms of haiku and tanka. There are also, some of the hip American poets of the era: Ginsberg, Kerouac, Pound, Bukowski, Braughtigan; but above all else, I have discovered Dylan Thomas; who is ever to grow in my esteem for his incomparable craft.

The poems vary in style and quality, with the occasional inspired moment; they are formative efforts but, like my hero, I am in love with words and how they might be assembled together (and, like my hero, I have a desire for a degree of obscurity). I think I glimpse Kathy in the rain on Putney Bridge, as I wait for my bus home to Kensington, one wet evening ... and I write a poem. I encounter a girlfriend from early university days out of nowhere on Victoria platform, briefly reconnect and then again lose touch ... and I write a poem. Young Scotsman Ron from the office noisily munches on an apple behind me ... and I write a poem. I take one of many train journeys for the office down to the steel fabricators in Exeter, on one particular rainy day ... and I write a lengthy poem, in tribute of a fashion, to Ginsberg. I lose my heart in an affair which I know cannot have any lasting future ... and I write many poems (which infatuation eventually will span some twenty years, to re-emerge in yet another larger batch of poems, when she briefly re-emerges in another place and time; mistaken for one cruel moment, as truly being the grail which was sought through all those years).

This affair, hopeless as it ultimately is destined to be, consists simply of a series of sweet but short, snatched moments in our own Camelot over the course of one gentle London spring, running into summer and linked together by the framework of a new but now-established friendship, which will itself remain discretely in the background over the many years to follow. Since it was never granted the opportunity to blaze fully, nor to be fully extinguished, its embers quietly glowed, occasionally fanned back to life during the course of the following years in different hemispheres, as she appeared and then disappeared again. It was in a sense, my own Fisher King moment and she, his mortal wounding. Eventually, the day would come when her role as the poet's muse, would be taken up by another; but much personal history and the attendant carrying of that wound would have to pass me by in the interim ... but those are other stories. Meanwhile, the poetry would continue to develop as knowledge, awareness and love for the art grew ... not in a continuous unbroken line but always moving steadily forward.

THE KEEPER

The keeper is lost –
And losing, so the unsheathed ring:
Time's annulary, bared in solemn gambit,
Gambled for an unseen queen –
She rings the pealing
Of the hours and houri, measured out upon
The bane Achilles held –
She keeps, and holding,
Holds his unkeeped heart
And bares it to the light of day.

The keeper is lost –
And keeping, keeps his solaced keep:
Kept high on castled crags, between the distance
Of his bursting soul's intent –
In his watch-housed sleep,
He's marked her measures;
Timed her hours of queen-shod waking –
For the outlawed swain, Astarte weep:
For he's pawned his heart
And bears it from the light of day.

Brad Drew © June 1976

MY FATHER'S GHOST: A MEMOIR

The Sydney Mews office, upstairs with my Miro / Calder Christmas mobile.

Sylvie, who waits outside a door and climbs through a window.
One Saturday morning at the Brick Lane Markets.

MY FATHER'S GHOST: A MEMOIR

Inside 20 Gordon Place, Kensington – small & modest, but comfortable: home.

20 Gordon Place, Kensington today ... Bill Squire's studio in the mansard. My flat behind the upper bay window (which Sylvie daringly scales).

Inside my flat at number 20.

A day at Canterbury & the Cathedral with Sooz (in foreground) and her sister.

The Barbican Development ... now heritage listed.
One of the residential towers hangs above the many apartment blocks –
ribbons of medium-rise residences topped by vaulted studio apartments.
The Arts Centre is gestating somewhere behind all this.

MY FATHER'S GHOST: A MEMOIR

12

The Last Days of London

ALL THINGS MUST END. Tony and Bodge Samson, when they finally leave with their boys to take up a new life in Fiji, hold a large farewell party at their flat in Pimlico, attended by all and sundry under the emblazoned banner of, 'Will the Last One out of London Please Turn Off the Lights!' It is a sometimes-wild and fun Last Hurrah. My final days are not so dramatically announced; there is no comet plummeting earthwards ... just a gentle and gradual signing off; ever with mixed feelings for the process and eventually, a great sadness which accompanies my final departure.

Wounding complete, I move on with life while continuing to quietly and privately continue what is now become a special, understanding friendship with my continuing muse. Freshly-arrived in this state of being, I travel with a friend whom she and I share (a fellow-Australian from the office), for a holiday in Italy; serving doubly as a holiday and a pleasant way to perform the necessity of renewing our visas. The plan had first been to fly to Pisa, for the Tower and then on to Florence. However, the airport at Pisa is closed at this time of year and so we settle for Venice as our entry point to Italy; this decision is a happy one, for it is Venice which personally impacts on me the most. We have heard the tales about how smelly Venice is. This, we find is not the case. The time is early spring, before the tourist season has started in earnest; and I imagine how perhaps, at the height of summer heat when the back lanes and canals are thick with tourists along with their thoughtlessly-discarded waste – then perhaps, it could smell and explain why most resident Venetians leave town for the season. What we find is sheer magic and enchantment; timelessness amongst the myriad of hidden lanes and alleyways, canals, brick and timber bridges large and small; where everywhere is heard the constant background of gentle water lapping and over all, falls the clean, pure smell of the untainted Adriatic sea.

We have a couple of days here before proceeding on to Florence. We share a small room in a pensione across the Grand Canal, not very far from the station and wander extensively; evening meals generally centre around fish dishes, which we drink with valpolicella; sip on tiny bottles of campari and soda with our expressos, as we observe the passing parade in St Mark's Square from the row upon row of small tables ranged all along one side of the piazza. Time passes quickly and we are soon back to the station for our train journey on to Florence. We have made no plans in advance for accomodation anywhere, since the season has not started and so, arrive for our five days in Florence, only to discover that it is the beginning of Saint Joseph's Weekend and practically every Tuscan from miles around is in the city for three days. We trudge from pensione to pensione, only to encounter 'al completo' at every turn. Finally, we find one address where the best that can be offered is in effect a five bed dormitory, with the warning that we may have to share it with others ... this happens before the day is out.

First to arrive are an American boy from Minnesota and a young Canadian travelling together, having met by chance in Morocco. The American tells the tale of their meeting there and of how he had written home to his mother to tell her of his new friend and to say that he was high in Morocco ... whereupon she reported to her ladies' tennis club with great pride, that her son was mountain-climbing in Morocco! It makes for a good story. Before the evening is out, we acquire our fifth occupant: a very immature young man from Florida, who is travelling with his girlfriend from home; she, being housed at this time in another part of the pensione. He speaks so disparagingly of her that we are all left wondering why on earth she bothers. The Americans and Canadian stay for only two nights but before our own five- night stay is over, we find ourselves sharing again; this time with three girls: an Australian and a New Zealander, along with another American.

Florence, as expected, is wonderful ... such a wealth of history, art and architecture. One walks everywhere, forever dodging the mosquito-like Vespas which buzz the cobbled streets and lanes. We visit the duomo, climbing up to the whispering gallery which encircles the inside base of the dome, a dizzying height above the floor below; and from there, we climb once again: this time, the enclosed, winding open steps lodged between the inner and outer brick domes, until at last, we find ourselves outside on the open terrace which sits over the dome and soars above the city, at the base of the grand lantern which crowns the cathedral. We visit the glorious Uffizi Gallery – and visit it again; nearby, the Piazza della Signoria and the Palazzo Vecchio with

Donatello's sensuous 'David' posing resplendent inside; the churches of Santa Croce and Santa Maria Novella, amongst others. We find the Academy Gallery with its towering Michaelangelo's 'David' dwarfing the viewer at the far end of a grand corridor, flanked by a haunting series of the great man's unfinished sculptures, where tortured figures struggle to break free of the marble which constrains them. We seek the Cimabue Crucifix at Santa Croce only to find that it remains inaccessible as it undergoes restoration following severe damage by the great floods of the Arno in 1966 ... these sensitive matters take time. We search for and find, 'Vivoli's': the most famous gelateria of the then-known world, and indulge ourselves.

Every day, just before Florence shuts down for the afternoon siesta, we stock-up with our lunch: a half-litre of Tuscany's famous but inexpensive 'Chianti', a loaf of crusty bread with a wedge of peppercorn parmesan, salami and olives – then, to cross the famous Ponte Vecchio and mount the slope up to the green lawns of the Giardino do Boboli, behind the Pitti Palace. There, we recline in splendid style, devouring our lunch at leisure, looking back over the city and either reading or writing letters home, or simply snoozing. One rainy afternoon, we attend a movie, only to discover that it is one which we had observed being filmed at one time previously, very near to our Sydney Mews office.

Before we came here, Andreas had told me how I simply must try the 'trippa' in Florence, since it is the national dish of Florence. I had grown up with tripe as a rather bland addition to the occasional family menu but nothing like this could have been imagined to spring from such a basic source of offal ... very Italian, with tomatoes, onion, carrot, celery and parmesan; and gently cooked to a melting tenderness. On our first night in the city, we happily discover a restaurant which is definitely a haunt of local families, rather than of tourists. We are tended by the head waiter, who almost does somersaults with pleasure when I request the 'trippa' for mains (fitted between a starter of fagioli with oil and garlic, followed by a runny slab of creamy dolcelatte for desert); thereafter, for the course of the evening, we receive royal service and when we go to settle the bill, find it to be considerably less than the menu would have indicated ... we have been granted the locals' charge rather than that for the tourists.

After five days of this, it is time to return to Venice for several more days in the city of enchantment. This time, we are even more relaxed and unhurried as we explore every little lane, alley, bridge and canal. Never do I recall feeling so ecstatic, entranced and purely happy at inhabiting a place, short as our stay might be. These final days cement a lifelong love-affair with this city of dreams, which pursues me, like my London muse, for all future time. My companion, Phil, is invaluable in Venice with his unerring sense of direction in this damp labyrinth of dead-end alleys (often watery), twisting lanes crossed overhead by lines of hanging washing, lost courtyards and hidden squares, bridges to nowhere and everywhere, where the slap of lapping water and muffled cries always manage to somehow sound distant, yet close by. Every other corner holds a new surprise as we suddenly come upon an equestrian statue or yet another forecourt to a church. We climb the clock tower adjacent St Mark's Basilica, to sit there on the roof at the foot of its large mechanical, moorish statues, as they swing their hammers to strike the hour above us. We walk the upper reaches of St Mark's amongst pungent clouds of incense, as the faithful attend mass down below us and the chanting of the service hangs in the clouds, glowing with the sunlight streaming in through the grand arched windows. We sip our campari in the Square and meander the Doge's Palace, to view the infamous Bridge of Sighs. We roam the light-filled interior of Santa Maria della Salute, observe beggars (an Indian woman with her little girl) on the steps of the

Rialto Bridge and find our way through the back-ways to The Arsenal and its Museum of Naval History. On our last day, we cross over the lagoon to the Lido on one of the older, open-bowed vaporettos and enjoy a light lunch at a table set out on the sandy shore. The weather is balmy, with a gentle breeze, as we make our return trip on the same water-bus. We stand up front on the open deck as the outlines of St Mark's, the square, the tower and the Palace of the Doge, gradually emerge from the haze before us and I find I have tears of joy, at the very beauty of it all, running quietly down my face. And I know I shall never get over the absolute magic of this water-borne City of Falling Angels, as John Berendt will somewhere in the future, describe it.

* * * * *

FOR NOW, THE RETURN TO LONDON with another twelve months securely on my visa, means a return to Gordon Place, Sydney Mews, Sir John Cass – and of being resigned to my Fisher King future. This is the summer of 1976 and of the accompanying heatwave conditions of record-breaking duration for the twentieth century in Britain. This is London, designed to withstand the chills of winter but poorly-equipped to survive the onslaught of unseasonal summers. This is a traditional architects' office of the mid-twentieth century ... we work over tracing paper on timber drawing boards with tee-squares and set-squares. Tracing paper is sensitive to humidity and moisture in all forms, and we perspire; there is no air-conditioning and life spent over the draughting board becomes difficult. Every afternoon, someone is nominated to collect money and visit the 'Samovar' cafe across the road to return with armloads of lemon sorbets. At lunch time, we collect a chilled bottle of white wine from the off-licence opposite and head down to the small churchyard on the way to King's Road; there, we strip down to our underclothes like the rest of the

English and sit about on the grass, sunning ourselves and sipping our wine over lunch.

By now, Bernard has left the office to return to his family in Worb, on the outskirts of Switzerland's administrative capital of Bern, where he works with his architect father. I make plans to visit him later in the year and to stay for a time with his family. In the interim, I acquire a new neighbour in the attic of number 22 Gordon Place. When I first meet her, Carmel is renting a room at my friends' house in Putney, having broken with the fellow who accompanied her from Sydney to London. She has an arts degree from Sydney University and is now studying spinning and weaving at the Camberwell College of Arts. Our meetings at the house are occasional in passing and, in the main, indifferent to each other; obviously intelligent and artistic, she can be entertaining and interesting on a range of subjects. One weekend at Putney, she informs me that she is moving into the house next door to mine and gives me her details. There begins a practice, when I am returning from my print-making at John Cass and if her attic light is on, of visiting her real-life garret and telling of my latest endeavours in the studio and displaying my efforts. This continues innocently and intermittently for weeks, until one evening, she pounces and my fate is sealed. In that moment, the plight of the Fisher King is laid aside; or at least accepted as unattainable, in the face of an alternative, attractive distraction ... laid aside, but never fully-forgotten, as the following years will one day, attest. In this state, I prepare to visit my good friend, Barmy Bernard Balmer from Bern.

* * * * *

IT IS LATE IN THE YEAR in the last weeks of autumn, when I arrive at Zurich airport, to be greeted joyfully by Bernard. His reports to me have been of continuing rain with cold weather and I have packed accordingly. When I arrive in Zurich, the rain stops and remains that way until my departure two weeks later. As he drives me back along the autobahn to Bern, he tells me of the structure and manner of the Swiss parliament in guaranteeing a direct democracy, which seems to be a more balanced arrangement in terms of fairly representing the will of the people overall, as opposed to the sometimes shortcomings of the Westminster system; he points out massive, heavily-grilled concrete openings in the sides of the mountains which we pass and explains how many of these mountains are hollowed out inside, stocked with supplies and essential services, such that in the event of invasion, the entire population can be safely stowed away in them within twenty-four hours and all the major highways detonated by the explosives already built into them (Switzerland being so totally mountainous, the only way of moving around the country is by the established road systems). We stop at one of the many roadhouses for our meal, while he continues to describe how all the internationally-famous Swiss banks have their vaults hundreds of metres underground, accessed only by lift shafts. The entire country begins to sound like the pristine precision workings of a giant Swiss watch.

The meals in the roadhouses and restaurants generally at this time of year, reflect a common seasonal theme: it is the height of the game season and is built around venison, wild boar and desserts based on variations of marron, mostly in the form of towering cones of piped marron (chestnut) puree. In one of the roadhouses we visit, the vast room is suddenly filled with the sound of competitive yodelling, one responding after another. Bernard explains how the men have yodelling clubs, which are really an excuse to get out for a night with the boys, enjoying a good meal and a boisterous singsong as they drink and dine. After the democratic manner of their parliament, where every citizen is given a voice in the running of the country and the passing of laws, so too is connubial arrangement of independent pieces of social life: the women attain balance in these times by having their sewing clubs, in which they manage their own nights out with the girls, wining, dining and gossiping into the small hours. It is all terribly conservative and village-like but civilised and balanced.

Bernard's family are warm and welcoming; his mother treats me like a second son. When I rise in the mornings, he and his father are already departed for the office. She has my breakfast of fresh bread with several cheeses and fresh coffee waiting for me and as I eat, she irons and we manage to talk of all manner of subjects from my life in Brisbane to the events of the flood; she knows virtually no English but some level of French along with her own Switzer-Deutsch, while my French remains sparse alongside my little-more-than schoolboy German ... yet somehow, we manage to cross-converse each morning, while she asks me what I plan to do that day.

Each day brings something new. I start with Bern itself and explore the Bahnhoff Strasse from its top to the Bear Plaza, Rose Garden and Deer Park at the very bottom of its steep slope. It is a very clever street ... one descends and ascends it under cover of continuous ground level arcading, where the footpath linking the shopfronts travels the distance as a series of long, very-gentle slopes connected by three or four steps each time across the full width of the footpath; the effect of this is that one can climb from the base to the summit of the street without ever being aware of the height scaled. As in many of these main station streets in Switzerland, a direct alternative path is to take the cable tramway which always runs down the centre of the street itself. In Zurich, I find that the footpath, kerb and street surface itself is clad in polished marble which fairly-glows under the street-lights after dark.

The brown bear of the Pyrenees is the national symbol of Bern and the Bear Plaza sits adjacent the bridge over the Aare River and contains accomodation for the large bears, opening out into the deep round pit with climbing platforms and arena, where the bears come out to play and entertain. They do seem to enjoy showing off to the crowds gathered around the balustrade above them, especially when fruit rewards are tossed by the tourists for them to cleverly catch and devour. In the current time, this has become a less Medieval arrangement for the bears, with a wide tunnel connecting their original playpen to a big, new natural parkland home; a true Bear Garden.

  I spend several scattered days exploring Bern itself, always pausing at an outdoor table in the busy Bahnhoff Plaza for an espresso, taken with my ever-present Gauloises or Gitanes, as I watch the Bernese street life pass by and wait to meet Bernard for lunch or else to move on to the next location of interest. In the days spread between these Bern ventures, I visit Zurich on a couple of occasions; discover Le Corbusier's only all-steel, pavilion building, completed after the architect's death and sitting in the parkland bounding Lake Zurich; view Chagall's stained glass chapel windows at the Fraumunster church and visit the Kunsthaus Museum. Throughout Zurich, in every little square, men play chess with giant pieces on equally-giant boards set into the pavement. In visiting the Grossmunster, I find myself deep in the crypt under the cathedral which houses a life-size wooden and heavily-weathered, ancient statue of Charlemagne. There are two more people down here with me in the bowels of the great church: a French woman who knows some English but virtually no German, a German who knows some French but no English, and myself, with my schoolboy German, limited French and of course, English. In spite of these differences, and by haltingly translating from one to the next in a common tongue and in a circular fashion, we manage to discuss Charlemagne and his place in history for around twenty minutes. I carry this experience away with me for all time, as one very-rich cross-cultural co-operative exchange. I should like to think that all three of us, there present that day, each remember the experience.

Other days, I visit Lucerne with its wonderful winding, covered bridge weaving its way across the lake and to Interlaken, on my way to the Bernese Oberland and the mountain pass of Kleine Scheidegg. One travels in stages to Kleine Scheidegg via a series of rail transports, finally with a steep rack-and-pinion tram ascent up the final grade. There at the crest, standing before the tourist information centre and restaurant/cafe, as I look out over crest upon crest of alpine peaks reaching forever before me, I cannot help but think that here in this spot, I stand on the top of the entire world, stretching out below. From here, one can see the Jungfrau and the Eiger. At one point in time, we hear a rumbling crash and look across to see the cloud of snow billowing up from where an avalanche has just occurred on an upper mountain slope. It is a special place, the day is sunny, crisp and clear and I feel almost overheated in my trendy Daniel Hechter light-weight wool suit ... and there are snow-capped peaks stretching out everywhere around me. I travel back the way I came and Interlaken itself is magical, as it lights up in the dusk.

On weekends, we visit Bernard's new girlfriend, Ruth, in Basel and stay over, dining with her brother, Kurt, at 'L' Escargot' - once again with lashings of venison following a truly-generous serving of traditional escargot. In the afternoon, we observe from a terrace high above the river, a wedding party as they cross from the opposite bank across the Rhine in an open barge, to land below us and ascend to the tree-shaded terrace where we and the other wedding guests stand. One weekend, we cross over the border into France, at Alsace, to wander the village we find there, close to the border; take coffee and pastries, then discretely enter a local vineyard as we return, to pluck an early grape or two from the vines we find there. Kurt is one of

Bernard's oldest friends and Bernard will, in a short while, marry his sister Ruth; who will in turn, remain a lifelong friend of myself, along with Bernard and their daughter, Annabel ... who will herself one day, become a forensic psychologist and a great pride to her parents.

All too soon, the visit approaches an ending. The weather throughout my stay has remained sunny and warm, just as I brought it with me. As Bernard drives me back up the autobahn to the airport and my flight home from Zurich, droplets of rain appear on the windscreen and build as we travel. By the time we reach the airport, it is raining in earnest and remains thus, for weeks after my return to London. It convincingly appears that I did bring the clear skies with me, only to take them back with me when I leave.

* * * * *

WHEN I ARRIVE back in London, my immigration experience takes on a new aspect as I encounter a female officer with a tougher-than-usual attitude to my status as a working holiday maker; previous entries had been friendly and the granting of a further twelve months on my visa had been an automatic response. Suddenly, there is a hint of aggression as she remarks, 'You're getting a bit old for this, aren't you?' (good grief, I'm only twenty-nine), as she stamps my passport for six months only. I am devastated.

For the past twelve months, I have been oscillating between writing my family and friends that I will be returning, at least for a while; shortly after, I cancel that forecast, as some new event overtakes and I decide to stay. Back home, the wedding preparations for number two sister, Glenys, have been underway for some time and are gathering pace. I do not really wish to leave London yet I do know that eventually, I must, since I do not hold residency status. I missed the qualifying grandparent condition by one generation and in ignorance, did not manage to pursue the acquisition of a work permit through the office, until it became too late (this, I only realise when Guillermo tells me that he has been finally granted residency status, after holding a work permit for the required three years). Had I known, I would have encouraged the office to seek one for me from the day when they first took me onboard full time.

Now, with the comment of the immigration officer ringing in my ears, I realise that I have little choice but to head home at last for the family wedding. I imagine that in six months perhaps, I might return and start over again. The senior people at Chamberlin Powell and Bon want me to return, which is an encouraging thought. I write home with my news of a definite return and they set their wedding date (an event which will take place on my thirtieth birthday ... for many ensuing years, I am to never receive birthday greetings from my sister, as she and her husband immerse themselves in their often-baby-making, anniversary celebrations – the coincidence of my birthday forgotten).

So, a new future course has been set. Carmel has plans herself, to return to her own family in Brisbane later in the year and we discuss setting up house together after that. Where that leads will be seen in the future; for the moment, it feels a good path to follow. I arrange my air ticket for June, at a good price on what turns out to be one of the last AUS (Australian Union of Students) jumbo flights out of London. Even so, I have to accept a loan from my father for the fare (something which he has previously offered and I, been too proud to accept). The costs of living, even modestly, in London during these years on the salary of a junior architect, have become increasingly difficult to maintain; even a senior staff member of the caliber of my good friend and immediate superior, John Connaughton has been feeling the pinch of austerity during these times.

There have been commiserations shared between us, musing over the occasional afterwork-Guinness and possibilities idly discussed for bolstering my sorry income. He relates how there had once been a student architect in the office, who had worked evenings as a male escort to expand his income; not a gigolo as such, but a paid escort. His clients primarily were single business women, in town for a short time and requiring someone to safely accompany them to dinner, shows or dancing. Asides from his fee from the agency, he was taken to the best restaurants, exclusive clubs and West End shows, often with a generous tip from the client herself if she enjoyed his company. Eventually, he escorts an American woman and her daughter to all the best places and they are so taken with him that they want to return to America with him.

This sounds so good to our naive young architect, that he compiles a list of the escort services spread through from Mayfair to Piccadilly over the weekend and, after work the following Monday, dressed in what he imagines to be his best summer outfit, he sets off on his mission to raise his living standards. From one address to the next through the backstreets of Mayfair, he discovers that most establishments deal exclusively in female escorts; the proprietress of one is currently doing time in prison and some are no longer to be found at all. His last port of call holds some hope of success: an establishment at the high end of Mayfair, close to Hyde Park Corner (presided over by a lady named Annina Spitzer), which does in fact, deal also in male escorts. As he approaches his goal, he is accosted by a security man bearing all the hallmarks of a retired policeman (which turns out to be accurately intuited), who proceeds to attempt to dissuade this young innocent from a depraved lifestyle ... by offering him work as a model for a gay magazine centred in Nottinghill Gate! He responds with the rejoinder that, if he is ever so desperate, he will look him up ... and so, he proceeds upstairs to the holding yard of

Mme Spitzer, where young women in various stages of undress lounge around, awaiting their assignments. This starts to feel a mite uncomfortable and when the lady herself arrives, she proclaims imperiously, 'Oh, my dear, but you're much too young!' Had I been suave, moustachioed and ten years older, I might have enjoyed some success in the venture. So much for that attempt to increase my fortunes (accompanied I confess, by some sense of relief) ... well, at least I tried.

Still desperate to increase my income, with the encouragement of my friend, I resolve to try my luck as a legitimate fashion model. I have my excellent camera and accessories; so, back in my flat, alone, I set up my camera on tripod with timer engaged and take a collection of black and white photographs in various outfits and settings. I do this and have the films developed but in the final analysis, I lack the self-confidence to take the project any further. As an egoist and narcissist, I am an abject failure. I should have waited for the age of social media ... but by then, I would be at my present age and state – all aesthetic appeal, null and void.

* * * * *

MY FINAL DAYS APPROACH as spring marks out her last days into summer. At Sir John Cass, Mirella has already departed with her family for a new life in Canada and Bonnie has moved on to her new life, or resumption of her old life, somewhere in the north of England; we all exchanged prints with each other as we headed our separate ways (Mirella and I continue by mail our exchanges of prints and our friendship until it finally runs out with time and distance). Bernard is back in Bern, while Pierre and Mary are, for the moment, back in Paris before the final move to New York. Phil has moved on, with his Texan lady, to America where he will operate his own small construction business for some years, before returning to Australia. Tony and Bodge have long-gone to the Pacific and Roddy has disappeared somewhere out of London. And there remains Carmel, due to follow me by year's end.

Naively, I reassure John Honor, our project architect at Sydney Mews and John Connaughton, that I shall return in six months time and am assured that my position will await me. On my last day at the office, I receive a farewell gift of a large book on David Hockney's art: a great favourite in these years. After work, the entire office sees me off in grand style with drinks in our local, at the entrance to the mews. I am touched to find that a large contingent from Lamont Road's head office have also come to farewell me. Everyone wants to buy drinks for me and follow one upon the other with their shouts; during these years, without conscious design or intent, I follow certain drink rituals – in flight, gin and tonic; at the theatre, campari, on the rocks or with soda; darts after work, Guinness; pub pool after work, cider; all other occasions, pastis: Pernod or Ricard. Not wishing to mix drinks, I insist on Pernod and ice ... and they keep coming such that our bartender makes life easier (?) eventually, by bringing out a ladies' Guinness goblet and adding each new 'shout', with ice, into it. Carmel, who is also there for the occasion, counts them off and informs me the following morning, when I can bear to face the light of day, that I have consumed fifteen of them before we leave for dinner with the remnants of our well-wishers. Guided by her, unsteadily, down the Fulham Road to our restaurant, I find great difficulty in articulating speech but find that I can speak quite legibly to her in ordering dinner, if I whisper ever so conspiratorially. It is a memorable send-off and a rewarding experience, even with the acute and delicate tenderness of the morning after.

The day has arrived. I am well-aware that loving family and friends dearly await my return and yet, I am filled by mixed emotions, which never seemed to occupy me when I first left home shore to come here. Whilst I have experienced moments of loneliness and touches of homesickness, this city has felt consistently more like home to me than any place I have ever been before. My bags are packed, some luggage sent on ahead and some overflow items stored with my friends, John and Sue, for my eventual return. All other friends still present, have been farewelled and nothing remains ... except London.

With mixed feelings and heavy heart, I set off for Heathrow. There is no turning back now. My luggage is stowed, I have my seat allocation and begin the long walk to the aircraft and the heartache of this final severance. The jumbo jet is lightly booked and little more than one third occupied. From where I sit in the aircraft, it feels like the empty lobby of a grand hotel before the season sets in ... I look forward and backwards into my nearest side aisle which curves away to infinity, revealing almost no sign of life – and so, it remains. I have the central row of five seats entirely to myself (which later, with arm rests elevated, makes for a fine bed to stretch out on, in my bereavement) and it is so very quiet. We slowly taxi towards my other home; we straighten up, pause and begin our sprint to the runway's end and liftoff.

There is a tangible, discernible moment when the first wheels, then the remainder, break contact with terra firma and clunk back so definitively into the undercarriage; the umbilical chord is severed and I am cast adrift ... and without knowing what I am doing, I sob.

London, Heathrow, 20 June 1977

MY FATHER'S GHOST: A MEMOIR

Venice: St Mark's Square & The Bridge of Sighs ...
The clocktower at St Mark's ... below which sits Phil at the striking of the hour.

MY FATHER'S GHOST: A MEMOIR

A hidden square in Venice on which I will later base a screen-print.

'Lost Dog Gothic': Screenprint 1982.
(Taken from the full-colour original.)

MY FATHER'S GHOST: A MEMOIR

The Duomo in Florence & the view from the top of the dome, below the lantern.

The Basilica of Santa Maria Novella, home of the famous Cimabue Crucifix. At this time, still being restored following the devastating inundation by the RiverArno in Florence, during the floods of 1966.

The Ponte Vecchio over the River Arno in Florence, from the upper Uffizi Gallery.

The deliberately-exaggerated perspective of the Uffizi Gallery with
The Palazzo Vecchio with the dome of The Duomo in background.

'Il Porcellino', bronze boar in the Mercato Nuovo, Florence: a bringer of good luck. (Forty-five years in the future, I shall rediscover another casting of this sitting in Macquarie Street, outside of Sydney Hospital: the city's earliest hospital).

The Schloss or Castle, in Worb, just outside of Bern where Bernard lives with his parents, in Switzerland.

MY FATHER'S GHOST: A MEMOIR

'The Rathaus', or Town-hall in Basle, Switzerland;
with Bernard & Ruth in Eggisheim, Alsace in France one Sunday afternoon.

The Jungfrau, at Kleine Scheidig, Switzerland.

MY FATHER'S GHOST: A MEMOIR

The last of 20 Gordon Place; Kensington, London, March 1997.

And it's goodbye from me: my aborted attempt at modelling ...
The last of nurturing Gordon Place, a farewell on the verge of June, 1977.

REAP THE MARCH WINDS

Reap the March winds
for a few days' madness –
steal the dead of night
from the Blind King's purse
and, singing in the madhouse heat,
reach out –
for she'll never come this way
again.

Brad Drew © March 1977

An Afterword:

So brief is this in fact, it resembles more of an Aside, rather than an Afterword. I'm aware that I am, in essence, an incurable romantic and sentimentalist ... always have been and not about to change. I took with me, an overwhelming sense of separation from this home of three years-plus and from one who had been my muse, in spirit at least, for the greater part of that time. I left, full of intent to return at the first opportunity but life intervened, as it has a habit of doing, usually so subtly that it is not fully-noticed ... and I never saw London again.

A pervasive homesickness for her, would regularly visit me with little provocation from conversation with others and my gentle muse would reappear at random intervals in my life over the years to come, reigniting the ever-present embers and eliciting new outpourings of the poetry which had been placed to one side. For some time, I would maintain a correspondence with the closest of those whom I had left behind. In time, they themselves would move on to new locations and new phases in their own lives and eventually, little by little, most of those connections would be lost along the way or unwittingly severed. As it is for the eventual fate of our earth's crust, time erodes ... and only the most durable rocks, those extruded from the depths, remain. So it would be with Bernard and Ruth; and so, for a very long time, with my reluctant butterfly of a muse.

To a large degree, even for the most self-directed, Fate holds the reins and none of us are ever truly, completely in control; even when we imagine that we are. It is probable that Dreamers are ever the least in control. I would move on through a series of other lives and continue to accept each as they happened. Eventually, even the sometimes-fateful muse of all those years would become lost to the erosion of uncompleted stories and another would emerge from the mists to claim her place, bringing forth poems at a new level. London, coupled with the love affair with Venice, would remain entrenched for all time; always calling but time and circumstance never permitting.

But that is all another story, best told another time.

MY FATHER'S GHOST: A MEMOIR

www.ingramcontent.com/pod-product-compliance
Lightning Source LLC
Chambersburg PA
CBHW070423010526
44118CB00014B/1871